The NCTE High School Literature Series

The NCTE High School Literature Series offers classroom teachers in-depth studies of individual writers. Grounded in theory, each volume focuses on a single author, work, or historical moment and features excerpts from writers' works, biographical information, and examples of student writing. The books provide rich opportunities for classroom discussion and writing assignments that teachers can adapt to their own literature curriculum.

Volumes in the Series

The Incarceration of Japanese Americans in the 1940s: Literature for the High School Classroom (2018), Rachel Endo

To Kill a Mockingbird *in the Classroom: Walking in Someone Else's Shoes* (2009), Louel C. Gibbons

Zora Neale Hurston in the Classroom: "With a harp and a sword in my hands" (2009), Renée H. Shea and [...]

Sherman Alexie in the Classroom: "...  *save our lives."* (2008), Heath[...] Christabel Umphrey

Tim O'Brien in the Classroom: "This[...] [...], Barry Gilmore and Alexander Kaplan

The Great Gatsby *in the Classroom: Searching for the American Dream* (2006), David Dowling

Judith Ortiz Cofer in the Classroom: A Woman in Front of the Sun (2006), Carol Jago

Langston Hughes in the Classroom: "Do Nothin' till You Hear from Me" (2006), Carmaletta M. Williams

Amy Tan in the Classroom: "The art of invisible strength" (2005), Renée H. Shea and Deborah L. Wilchek

Raymond Carver in the Classroom: "A Small, Good Thing" (2005), Susanne Rubenstein

Sandra Cisneros in the Classroom: "Do not forget to reach" (2002), Carol Jago

Alice Walker in the Classroom: "Living by the Word" (2000), Carol Jago

Nikki Giovanni in the Classroom: "The same ol danger but a brand new pleasure" (1999), Carol Jago

The Incarceration of Japanese Americans in the 1940s

Literature for the High School Classroom

The NCTE High School Literature Series

Rachel Endo

University of Washington Tacoma

NATIONAL COUNCIL OF TEACHERS OF ENGLISH
1111 W. KENYON ROAD, URBANA, ILLINOIS 61801-1096

Staff Editor: Bonny Graham
Interior Design: Jenny Jensen Greenleaf
Cover Design: Lynn Weckhorst
Cover Image: Library of Congress, Prints & Photographs Division, FSA/OWI Collection, LC-DIG-fsa-8a31193

NCTE Stock Number: 22983; eStock Number: 23003
ISBN 978-0-8141-2298-3; eISBN 978-0-8141-2300-3
ISSN 1525-5786

Library of Congress Cataloging-in-Publication Data

Names: Endo, Rachel, author.
Title: The incarceration of Japanese Americans in the 1940s : literature for the high school classroom / Rachel Endo, University of Washington Tacoma.
Description: Urbana, Illinois : National Council of Teachers of English, [2018] | Series: The NCTE high school literature series | Includes bibliographical references. |
Identifiers: LCCN 2017054987 (print) | LCCN 2018012073 (ebook) | ISBN 9780814123003 () | ISBN 9780814122983 (pbk.)
Subjects: LCSH: Japanese Americans—Evacuation and relocation, 1942–1945—Study and teaching (Secondary) | Japanese American literature—Study and teaching (Secondary) | Japanese Americans in literature. | World War, 1939–1945—United States—Literature and the war.
Classification: LCC D769.8.A6 (ebook) | LCC D769.8.A6 E65 2018 (print) | DDC 940.53/1773089956—dc23
LC record available at https://lccn.loc.gov/2017054987

In loving memory of Ojiisan *(Endo Takashi) and Peter T. Suzuki*

Permission Acknowledgments

Contents

■■■■■■■■■■■■■■■■■■■■■■■■■■■■■■■■

Acknowledgments xi

1. Why Japanese American Literature? 1

2. Essential Background Information and Context 13

3. Jeanne Wakatsuki Houston's *Farewell to Manzanar* . . . 26

4. Teaching *Farewell to Manzanar* on Screen 58

5. Lawson Fusao Inada's Poetry 84

6. Hisaye Yamamoto's Short Stories 112

7. Connecting Japanese American Literature to Current
   Events 138

Annotated Bibliography 145

Works Cited 151

Author 161

Acknowledgments

■ ■

I am honored to have this book published by the National Council of Teachers of English. I thank Bonny Graham and the NCTE Editorial Board, as well as the anonymous reviewers, for all of their helpful feedback on the manuscript. I am especially grateful to the hundreds of aspiring and current teachers, teacher educators, and young people who helped me test out the various activities and ideas mentioned in this book. Everyone's critical and thoughtful feedback helped me create a guidebook that I believe will be of great use to teachers of English.

I have many people to thank for their ongoing support of my scholarly endeavors. From the University of Nebraska at Omaha: Shereen Bingham, John Christenson, Joong-Gun Chung, Julia Garrett, the late John Langan, Sue Maher, Gary Marshall, Jody Neathery-Castro, Saundra Shillingstad, and Phil Smith, among many others, are the core people who helped me launch several lifelong dreams. From the University of Illinois at Urbana–Champaign, I thank my friends and mentors for helping me develop my identity as an ethnic studies scholar: Diem-My Bui, Mary Ellerbe, Violet J. Harris, Sharon S. Lee, Shelley S. Lee, Kent Ono, and Yoon Pak. From Hamline University: Colleen Bell, Veena Deo, Frank Hernandez, the late Subira Kifano, Fayneese Miller, John Pyle, Mike Reynolds, Naomi Taylor (Julia and Willie), and Sheila Wright all helped me more critically articulate what it means to be an ethnic studies scholar in education. Special thanks to Bill Lindquist for stepping in during my sabbatical to allow me to finish the bulk of this project.

Vichet Chhuon helped me locate several rare sources for this project. Special thanks to Bette-B Bauer, Karla Bergen, Sr. Judy Eby, Kevin Kumashiro, J. B. Mayo, Sue Schlichtemeier-Nutzman, Stanley I. Thangaraj, and Annette Wannamaker for their kindness and support of me over the years. Finally, I thank my parents, Endo Tsutomu and Endo G., as well as the rest of my extended and immediate families, for tolerating my crazy ideas and wild dreams.

1 Why Japanese American Literature?

■ ■

After the September 11, 2001, terrorist attacks in New York City, some American journalists and political leaders commented that "another Pearl Harbor" had occurred. In the name of national security, the US government began increasing its surveillance efforts at all levels from local mosques to international airports. Then-President George W. Bush and other political leaders defended their action as a necessary means to prevent future acts of terrorism. In response to this grand plan, national organizations such as the Japanese American Citizens League (JACL), founded in 1929 and the oldest Asian American civil rights organization in the United States, began to release public statements that strongly condemned what they saw as racist counterterrorism political projects. The JACL joined an American Civil Liberties Union lawsuit that challenged the premise of the USA Patriot Act (the Uniting and Strengthening America by Providing Appropriate Tools Required to Intercept and Obstruct Terrorism Act of Congress, signed into law October 2001) by stating that its scope of surveillance activities violated all Americans' civil liberties and constitutional rights. The JACL also began to compare the events leading to the mass incarceration of Japanese Americans in the 1940s and the racialization of Arab Americans, Muslim Americans, and South Asian Americans as extremists and terrorists in the post-2001 era. While receiving initial backlash for promoting what was seen

1

by some political leaders as unpatriotic views, the message soon gained traction as more Americans became disillusioned by the emotional toll and financial costs associated with President Bush's Global War on Terrorism.

In the early 2000s, I was among a handful of educators of color in Nebraska and also an active member of JACL. After giving a speech about the politics of wartime hysteria at the University of Nebraska Omaha, I started receiving invitations to visit K–12 classrooms and teacher preparation programs to discuss how the mass detainment of Japanese Americans in the 1940s had implications for current conversations about racial profiling in times of heightened concerns about America's safety and security. The timing was significant given what was making local and national headlines: a local mosque was receiving threatening messages from an anonymous caller, and the systemic abuse and torture of detainees at the Abu Ghraib prison by American soldiers was cycling in the daily news. Many Americans also expressed outrage that so-called extra security measures such as enhanced airport screenings disproportionately targeted and criminalized persons with certain physical features, religious affiliations, and surnames.

One particular student-led dialogue continues to remind me of the value of encouraging young adults to see connections between current events and history through the lens of ethnic literature. In 2003, I visited a twelfth-grade English teacher's classroom to teach Miné Okubo's (1946/2003) *Citizen 13660,* a graphic novel of 189 drawings with accompanying text chronicling the author's life in detainment in the 1940s. I started our class by reading part of the preface: "In the history of the United States this was the first mass evacuation of its kind in which civilians were removed simply because of their race" (pp. viii–vix). Before facilitating a whole-group discussion, I had students discuss with one another their

2

immediate reactions to this quote in relation to what they were hearing in the news about various counterterrorism efforts. What unfolded were several compelling conversations and competing perspectives about the government's responsibility regarding balancing individuals' civil liberties against larger concerns with preserving national security.

Pete, a White American male student, started the conversation: "I don't see the problem [with] extra screening. If someone 'looks' suspicious, they should be prepared to answer questions about who they are and their motives. It's better to be safe than sorry." A few other students chimed in to affirm Pete's stance. However, Fatima, an Egyptian American student who didn't wear a hijab and who also identified as Muslim, countered: "It's easy for you to say those things when you're not personally affected. And what does it mean exactly to 'look' suspicious?" After Fatima shared her experience growing up in an immigrant family that at different points and in various contexts could or couldn't "pass" as Arab, Muslim, or White, other students began to question the premise of racial profiling under the guise of national security. Christina, a Mexican American student, shared what it was like for her family to experience constant harassment, including being called "illegals" by some of their White American neighbors with threats to turn them in to law enforcement simply because of their skin color and surname. From there, we were able to discuss various elements of *Citizen 13660,* including connecting it to students' personal experiences and various current events that concerned them.

With the right framing, ethnic literature offers multiple avenues for young adults like Christina, Fatima, and Pete to explore critical questions about what's at stake for all Americans when certain groups are targeted, segregated, and socially excluded because of their assumed or real social identities. Japanese American literature from the World War II era specifically surfaces a relatively invisible moment in our nation's history while offering students critical counterperspectives about what it means to be "American." For example, excerpts from Okubo's *Citizen 13660* (2003) speak to "right the wrong done during the war," and telling "the shocking story" (p. xii) of what happened to Japanese Americans in the 1940s to illuminate the histories and literatures of ethnic Americans is usually not part of the regular curriculum. The writings of Okubo and other Japanese American authors also connect to contemporary examples of social injustice that are eerily similar to past histories when we analyze the uneven legal protections that different Americans are afforded depending on factors such as disability, gender, race, religion, and sexual orientation.

Having written the bulk of this book before the 2016 US presidential election, I now see with even greater clarity that Japanese American literature is a particularly relevant vehicle for discussing current events and social issues with young adults. Controversial rhetoric, proposals, and policies have received considerable attention since President Donald J. Trump's inauguration, including his plans to build a wall along the Mexican–US border, emboldening Immigration and Customs Enforcement (ICE) agents to detain people whose immigration status is in question, and his push to implement Executive Order 13769, also infamously known as the travel ban that targets Muslim-majority nation-states. Teachers across the United States have been fielding questions from their students about how Trump's policies might impact their classmates and their own families. In the aftermath of the 2016 US presidential election, for example, several teachers in New York City Public Schools, such as English teacher Kevin Kearns, allowed their students, many from immigrant and refugee families, to discuss their reactions to the election, including sharing their concerns about the fate of their futures as gendered and racialized Americans (Fertig & Khan, 2016). Thus, studying Japanese American history and literature clearly has relevance to the state of twenty-first-century America in an intensely contested and hostile political climate.

As a note of caution, it would be problematic to attribute postmodern racist and xenophobic policies to the Trump administration alone, or to point blame to one political party for perpetuating racially oppressive laws. Different leaders across the political divide have responded to wartime hysteria in predictable and unpredictable ways. However, any conversation with K–12 students about government-sanctioned racial profiling and racism will be controversial, especially when dominant messages of American exceptionalism under the guise of national security and patriotic duty are still widely promoted in the aftermath of a major political crisis. In times of heightened political tension, young adults need to think critically about what America stands for, and to reflect on why the United States remains a racially contested society even decades after the passage of major reforms related to civil rights and equal access to public services. In times of political fear and uncertainty, teachers have multiple opportunities to create inclusive spaces for young adults to engage in courageous conversations about the past and present state of America, and to imagine what it'd take to ensure that we live in a future free of hatred and violence.

Purpose and Scope

Encompassing diverse forms, genres, and perspectives, Japanese American literature has been in existence since the late 1930s (Chin, 1991). Japanese American literature could be defined as works written about, by, and/or for Japanese Americans, although the most widely recognized titles are based on the World War II incarceration of Japanese Americans. Prominent Japanese American authors such as Jeanne Wakatsuki Houston, Lawson Fusao Inada, Lonny Kaneko, John Okada, Miné Okubo, Monica Itoi Sone, Yoshiko Uchida, Mitsuye Yamada, and Hisaye Yamamoto were all children and young adults when their families were incarcerated in the 1940s. They've written memoirs, novels, picture books, poems, and short stories based on their direct and indirect memories of the World War II era as young Americans who experienced intense racial intolerance during times of extreme anti-Asian sentiment.

The study of Asian American literature, especially works by Japanese Americans, became more prominent at US colleges and universities on the West Coast in the 1970s during the rise of various ethnic studies movements. However, both in the 1970s and now in the twenty-first century, most Americans, particularly K–12 students living outside of the West Coast, haven't been regularly introduced to the works of Japanese Americans or other Asian American writers. *The Incarceration of Japanese Americans in the 1940s: Literature for the High School Classroom* offers teachers tools to diversify their Eurocentric secondary literature curriculum by focusing on incorporating literature about the World War II incarceration of Japanese Americans. The focus on this historical moment is intentional, as the illegal incarceration of Japanese Americans in the 1940s represents "one of the most troublesome instances of government-sanctioned mass incarceration, racial profiling, and segregation in U.S. history" (Endo, 2012, p. 17).

Each chapter provides essential contextual information to guide teachers in constructing culturally relevant and engaging lessons focused on select works of Japanese American literature. My representative examples are from three critically acclaimed Japanese American authors—Jeanne Wakatsuki Houston, Lawson Fusao Inada, and Hisaye Yamamoto. These authors were children or young adults in the early 1940s when their families were stripped of their constitutional rights, racially profiled, and subsequently detained in government-sponsored concentration camps. While their works represent different gendered and generational perspectives, their writings are unified around the theme of reviving memories of some of the darkest years in American history.

Chapter 1 provides a brief overview of Asian American (specifically, Japanese American) experiences in the United States, along with guidelines for appropriate use of language and terminology. Chapter 2 describes the formation and transformation of Japanese American literature around key moments in Asian American history. This chapter also offers a range of prereadings and prior-knowledge activities for teachers to help prepare students for more extensive study of Japanese American literature. Chapter 3 focuses on teaching Wakatsuki Houston's critically acclaimed memoir, *Farewell to Manzanar* (*FWTM*), along with ideas to help secondary students write their own identity-based mini-memoirs. Chapter 4 includes similar ideas for teaching the film version of *FWTM*. Chapter 5 delves into Inada's poetry by analyzing how his works address the relationship between historical trauma and racial inequities, as well as spotlighting the intriguing parallels he draws between Japanese American and American Indian cultures and histories. Also included are Inada-inspired ideas for encouraging students to write and share their own poems. Chapter 6 provides several frameworks for teaching Yamamoto's short stories, including thematic connections to the works of other major American women writers. Chapter 7 offers different strategies and topics for linking Japanese American literature to current events in the United States.

Why Japanese American Literature?

Situating Japanese American literature as part of the field of American literature rather than international or world literature is an essential point for teachers to establish early on with their students. Interestingly, students are often surprised when I proclaim: "Japanese Americans are Americans, not foreigners from Japan." Much of their surprise could be due to the reality that Asian American experiences, histories, and identities are still relatively absent from the official K–12 curriculum across content areas and grade levels. Some teachers also don't differentiate between the study of Asians in Asia and Asian Americans in the US context, including in their selection of curricular materials, which often confuses students about whether certain ethnic and racialized Americans like Japanese Americans are actually American. The first point that I reiterate with students is that Asian Americans are indeed American, while also challenging them to ponder why factors such as ethnicity, national origin, and race still determine who's represented in the K–12 curriculum as American citizens, noncitizens, and second-class citizens.

Although they've been in the United States for many generations, Asian Americans have long struggled to claim America as their own. The US Congress passed a resolution in 1978 to establish Asian Pacific American Heritage Week to honor this diverse community's many unsung contributions to our nation. Fourteen years later, in 1991, President George H. W. Bush proclaimed the month of May as Asian Pacific American Heritage Month ("May Is Asian/Pacific American Heritage Month," 2012). With a four-decade history of bipartisan national recognition, one might assume that in the twenty-first century, more US K–12 schools and universities have, at a minimum, formally acknowledged the contributions of diverse Asian Americans through curricular and extracurricular integration. Unfortunately, because of the deeply ingrained assumption that they're relatively new Americans who haven't experienced wide-scale racial discrimination, Asian Americans are still often absent from conversations and lessons on multiculturalism. Such an assumption fuels the unfortunate myth that Asian Americans are "illegitimate Americans" (Tuan, 1998, p. 37) while also erasing their long histories in the Americas that have been defined by racially exclusionary and segregationist moments.

As a Japanese American educated in predominantly White public schools and taught by all-White teachers at the beginning of these federally designated efforts to recognize ethnic and racial diversity, I learned nothing about Asian Americans and very little about diverse perspectives during my K–12 schooling. A few of my English teachers incorporated literature written by White women such as Louisa May Alcott, Jane Austen, Kate Chopin, and George Eliot to teach about what they considered diverse perspectives beyond White male authors, but within this narrow framework, there was little mention of authors of color, and Asian American authors were nonexistent. As a preservice education major at the University of Nebraska Omaha, I finally learned about ethnic literature in a Survey of American Literature course. The professor, a White American male with progressive views about inclusive education, introduced us to the writings of Sandra Cisneros, Sui Sin Far, Jeanne Wakatsuki Houston, Langston Hughes, Maxine Hong Kingston, Toni Morrison, Leslie Marmon Silko, and Amy Tan, among others. This was the first and only class in my entire K–16 experience in which ethnically and racially diverse authors, including various Asian American writers, were included as a part of, rather than apart from, the canon.

However, teaching American literature from multicultural perspectives is still more the exception than the rule. Despite their long history in America, in addition to a population increase in US K–12 schools of 46 percent since 1997 (Krogstad & Fry, 2014), Asian Americans continue to remain relatively invisible in the classroom. When I teach lessons and units on Japanese American literature in K–12 or university settings, it's often the first and only introduction that students will have to learning about Asian Americans' experiences in and contributions to the United States. Even today, I meet hundreds of students, including young Asian Americans, who haven't read one book by an Asian American author by the time they graduate from high school or their postsecondary institution. This is common even in progressive schools or universities that publicly promote missions of diversity, equity, and multicultural education.

My focus on Japanese American literature offers an admittedly incomplete picture of Asian America's vast literary contributions. For one, Japanese Americans represent only one of Asian America's more than two dozen government-designated ethnic groups. Hundreds of works authored by ethnically diverse Asian American writers such as Chinese American Gene Luen Yang, Filipino American Carlos Bulosan, Hmong American Kao Kalia Yang, Korean American Linda Sue Park, and Vietnamese American Thanhha Lai, among others, are also worthy of study in the classroom. Second, as not all Japanese Americans have familial connections to the World War II incarcerations, teaching about this historical moment can't and shouldn't be the only representation of Japanese American experiences. For example, while I'm Japanese American, my family's history doesn't include being incarcerated during World War II. However, learning about the World War II incarceration through the lens of Japanese American literature has shaped my own identity as a critical multicultural educator who believes that introducing young adults to diverse perspectives is essential in developing socially conscious citizens.

Japanese American literature also serves broader pedagogical purposes beyond introducing our students to Japanese American history. Given that diversity, identity, and race relations in America tend to be framed according to the Black–White racial binary, teachers certainly "need to expand our vision of what the canon should be, recognizing that the canon needs to make room for authors beyond that of the usual Caucasian and African American selections" (Chiu, 1997, p. 30). Introducing Japanese American literature to students as either a comparative or a stand-alone unit is just one of many ways to provide them with more inclusive models and representations of American history, identity, and literature. In addition to providing culturally and historically specific stories, Japanese American literature speaks to universal human experiences that young adults readily relate to, including dealing with conflict, living through regret, and surviving challenging life experiences such as death or other kinds of loss. While this book doesn't offer a comprehensive overview of Asian American literature, it provides essential background information about how to incorporate the historical literature of one ethnic group, Japanese Americans, into the secondary literature classroom.

Connections to the Common Core State Standards

The content of this book aligns with the instructional objectives common in the secondary language arts curriculum, offering differentiated and student-friendly activities and assignments that could be easily applied to the literature of other ethnic groups.

Recognizing the growing expectation that today's high school students should graduate with a range of knowledge and skills, this book incorporates several of the Common Core State Standards for English Language Arts (CCSS ELA) spanning grades 9–12. By 2015, several states had adopted all or parts of the CCSS ELA standards, which significantly overlap with the content standards set forth by most state departments of education. To capture key overarching competencies, the activities and assignments in this book infuse core aspects of the CCSS ELA standards for grades 9–12 with an integrated focus on the seven characteristics of college-ready students: that they (1) demonstrate independence as learners, (2) build strong interdisciplinary content knowledge, (3) respond to varying demands and tasks, (4) are able to comprehend as well as critique information, (5) value and incorporate evidence, (6) use technology and digital media effectively and responsibly, and (7) come to understand other perspectives and cultures (NGA Center & CCSSO, 2010, p. 7). Rather than focusing on single standards, however, this book uses an interdisciplinary, integrated, and multistandards approach that can be adjusted to meet varied learning outcomes and pedagogical goals. All of the activities, assignments, and readings have been designed to assist teachers as they develop their own interdisciplinary approaches to teaching different genres of Japanese American literature.

2 Essential Background Information and Context

This chapter focuses on central moments in Asian American history to situate the key events that led to the mass incarceration of Japanese Americans in 1942, which will provide essential information for teachers to understand the sociocultural and sociopolitical contexts for teaching ethnic literature, specifically Japanese American literature, in the secondary classroom. I briefly discuss appropriate terminology and the power of language in order to provide guidance on how to encourage students to negotiate potentially challenging conversations about how Japanese Americans and other racialized Americans have experienced racism over time. At the same time, I'm not claiming this is the only way to teach American ethnic literature, nor am I trying to discourage critical dissent or divergent viewpoints in the classroom. Several teachers have shared that all of this information has helped them avoid unintentionally teaching culturally insensitive, incomplete, or inaccurate information about Japanese American experiences and identities.

Terminology and the Power of Language

Language matters. When reading ethnic literature about certain historical moments, especially those pertaining to a group's experiences with racial discrimination, the appropriate use of labels and terminology should be clarified during the first class to set the stage for students to engage in culturally sensitive analyses and discussions. As Harris (2003) reminds us, "Naming is clearly political and indicative of the power (or lack thereof) wielded by a group" (p. 118). The politics of language is a particularly sensitive issue for Japanese Americans because much controversy over the past several decades has surrounded the language and theories used to describe their experiences before and during World War II.

I always address the politics and power of language use with students to help them identify the various gaps, imbalances, and omissions in mainstream representations of Japanese American experiences in history and literature. Students read and discuss the *Power of Words Handbook: A Guide to Language about Japanese Americans in World War II: Understanding Euphemisms and Preferred Terminology*, a short publication released by the Japanese American Citizens League (2013). This concise booklet offers detailed summaries of the different types of definitions, phrases, and words to be aware of when learning or teaching about Japanese American experiences and histories. As a prominent example, the word *internment* is most often used both outside and within the Japanese American community to describe the confinement of Japanese Americans during World War II. Its use, however, like the words *evacuation* and *relocation,* is contested. In my conversations with students and teachers, I specifically reference the "Terminology" (n.d.) section of the Denshō Japanese American Legacy Project to address the necessity of using direct, historically accurate, and precise language:

> The commonly used term "internment" is misleading when describing the concentration camps that held 120,000 people of Japanese descent during the war. "Internment" refers to the legally permissible detention of enemy aliens in time of war. It is

problematic when applied to American citizens; yet two-thirds of the Japanese Americans incarcerated were U.S. citizens. (n.p.)

Roger Daniels (1998), a historian who has written extensively about Japanese American history, explains how the terms *concentration camp, confinement, detention, imprisonment, incarceration, racial profiling,* and *segregation* more accurately represent the experience of incarcerated Japanese Americans during World War II. To address the concerns raised by descendants of Holocaust survivors regarding these same word choices, he recommends that we specifically refer to the sites where European Jews were exterminated as *death* or *extermination camps* rather than as *concentration camps.* I always use the recommended definitions and terms reiterated by Daniels (1998, 2002, 2005), which Denshō ("Terminology," n.d.) also supports in its historical and scholarly analysis of the legal and physical environment that Japanese American detainees confronted during World War II:

> In fact, they were prisons—compounds of barracks surrounded by barbed wire fences and patrolled by armed guards—which Japanese Americans could not leave without permission. "Relocation center" inadequately describes the harsh conditions and forced confinement of the camps. As prison camps outside the normal criminal justice system, designed to confine civilians for military or political purposes on the basis of race and ethnicity, these so-called relocation centers also fit the definition of "concentration camps." (n.p.)

When reading Japanese American literature, readers are likely to encounter contradictory terms such as *Japanese, Japanese American,* or, worse yet, the pejorative *Jap* or *Oriental.* As an adjective, *Japanese* should be used to reference the culture and language.

As a noun, *Japanese* can be used to describe a native of Japan or a Japanese immigrant. *Japanese American* is an all-encompassing term that refers to immigrants and their American-born descendants. Similarly, *Asian American* is a pan-ethnic umbrella label that includes Americans from diverse Asian ancestries, including those who identify as Cambodian, Chinese, Filipina/Filipino, Hmong, Indian, Japanese, Korean, Laotian, or Vietnamese, among others (Espiritu, 1992). The terms *Jap* and *Oriental* are unacceptable for modern-day usage, although they may appear in original texts written by Japanese American authors and in primary sources from earlier times such as government documents and newspaper articles.

Gathering Prior Knowledge

While most students I've worked with haven't learned about Japanese American history during their K–12 years, I still find it essential to gather information about their prior assumptions and knowledge to determine how much background information they'll need before we start to read a text. Figure 2.1 provides a sample group K-W-L chart that teacher candidates I worked with created and that we piloted in a tenth-grade English classroom. Sample answers with follow-up reflections from students are provided in each column. An extra Column D could pose the question, "What more do you want to learn?" This chart could be easily reproduced on a blackboard, whiteboard, or poster board; some of my students have shared a Google Doc to type in their answers in real time while we debrief as a whole group.

A. What do you **K**now about Japanese Americans in terms of their experiences in the United States?	B. What do you **W**ant to know about Japanese Americans in terms of their experiences in the United States?	C. What key points did you **L**earn? What, if anything, surprised you?
The Japanese had a difficult time when they first came here.	Why did they come to America? When?	The Meiji Restoration in Japan pushed lower-class Japanese to America. Most Japanese immigrants who came to the US from the 1890s–1920s worked in the agriculture industry or other low-wage jobs. Japanese immigrants weren't allowed to become citizens because of anti-Asian citizenship laws. Their American-born children were also seen as foreigners because of their race.
The Japanese were imprisoned during World War II.	Why were they imprisoned?	President Franklin D. Roosevelt authorized the imprisonment of Japanese Americans in 1942. Most Japanese Americans were American citizens. The US government didn't have clear evidence to put Japanese Americans into the camps.

Continued on next page

Figure 2.1. K-W-L chart for gathering information about students' prior knowledge.

Figure 2.1. Continued.

		German American and Italian American citizens weren't put into camps. A smaller number of German and Italian nationals were interned but not on a large scale.
Seems like they're very successful and hardworking.	I want to know what makes them so successful.	"Model minority" is the name of a common stereotype about Asian American people. It has a grain of truth . . . but it's often used to make claims that other minorities aren't as hardworking. This can lead to tension between Asians and other minorities. Many Asian families feel that they have to live up to this stereotype. Many teachers might assume that all Asians are good at math. It can cause a lot of stress for their children.
They come from very traditional cultures.	How does assimilation impact their understanding of American and Japanese culture? What types of cultural conflicts do Japanese American children confront?	Japanese Americans are diverse like any other group. Assimilation doesn't impact everyone in the same way. Some Japanese Americans have experienced internalized oppression and self-hatred. However, others have radical political viewpoints and have challenged racism.

Continued on next page

Figure 2.1. Continued.

	What cultural barriers do Japanese American girls face in American society?	Japanese culture in itself isn't necessarily patriarchal. All cultures have gender bias and prejudice, but Western culture tends to focus on gender discrimination in other cultures. World War II traumatized many Japanese Americans. Several wanted to "prove" their loyalty and patriotism by shedding their Japanese culture and identity.

Establishing Context: A Brief Overview of Japanese American History

After analyzing key trends from the K-W part of the K-W-L activity, I provide a brief overview of Japanese American history to prime students for subsequent activities and discussions. I suggest that teachers who would like to provide their students with outside pre-reading assign *A Troubling Legacy: Anti-Asian Sentiment in America* (JACL, 2005). This short, sixteen-page booklet, freely available online, provides a concise but detailed overview of the nature and scope of anti-Asian sentiment in the United States before and after the 1940s. Many sections specifically address how the World War II incarceration impacted Japanese Americans before, during, and after the 1940s. I also ask students to identify common themes from *A Troubling Legacy* that cut across the experiences of early Chinese, Filipino, and Japanese immigrants. We connect how anti-Asian sentiment continues to impact Asian American communities and individuals in the twenty-first century. We also comparatively analyze how racism and xenophobia uniquely impacted different Asian-origin groups across generations and regions, as well as other immigrant and refugee groups that have arrived in the United States more recently.

While some teachers may prefer to create their own slideshow presentations to efficiently convey in one class period the key points discussed in the following sections, I have, time permitting, asked students to research specific events, laws, or topics in preparation for in-class historical reenactments that could include short audiovisual presentations. PBS Learning Media offers options for teachers to create their own interactive storyboards or to assign students the task of creating their own: www.pbslearningmedia .org/tools/storyboard/. This platform also allows teachers to attach assignments and quizzes to the storyboards, and to track student completion. Whether I present the information myself or assign students in pairs or small groups to do their own research, I find it helpful to cover the following events, laws/acts, and people (see Figure 2.2). The next section provides additional details and

Before WW II	During WW II	After WW II
1. Chinese Exclusion Act (1882) 2. Gentlemen's Agreement Act (1907) 3. *Ozawa v. United States* (1922) 4. Immigration Act (1924)	1. Executive Order 9066 (1942) 2. *Yasui v. United States* (1943) 3. *Hirabayashi v. United States* (1943) 4. Ex parte Mitsuye Endo (1944) 5. *Korematsu v. United States* (1944)	1. Immigration and Nationality Act, also known as the McCarran-Walter Act (1952) 2. Establishment of the Commission on Wartime Relocation and Internment of Civilians or CWRIC (1980) 3. The murder of Vincent Chin (1982) 4. Civil Liberties Act (1988)

Figure 2.2. Sample informational table for organizing background information.

explanations about core themes in Japanese American history that help to establish the appropriate context for reading Japanese American literature.

A History of Exclusion

Japanese Americans have had a relatively long presence in the Americas as one of Asian America's most established ethnic groups. However, during the early to mid-1900s, Asian nationals in North America experienced a variety of barriers that prevented them from obtaining the legal, political, and social rights that were available or more accessible to their European counterparts. Based on anxiety about and aversion to the racially different, White American political leaders institutionalized a race-based classification system in which Asian nationals were identified as "aliens ineligible for citizenship" and subsequently excluded from equal protection under the law (Ngai, 2005, p. 26). Racially charged Yellow Peril rhetoric depicted early Asian nationals and their descendants as culturally deviant and un-American foreigners.

Long before they were incarcerated in the 1940s, Japanese Americans experienced extreme forms of discrimination and prejudice. Since the first arrivals of Japanese immigrants to the United States in the late 1800s, "White workers resented not only Japanese competition but their very presence in America" (Takaki, 1989, p. 198). Anti-Japanese sentiment only intensified after Japan attacked Pearl Harbor on December 7, 1941, which negatively affected public perceptions of Japanese Americans—including those who were born and raised in the United States. Managed by the War Relocation Authority (WRA), more than 110,000 Japanese Americans from California, Oregon, and Washington were rounded up and then detained in ten concentration camps located in harsh, desolate, and uninhabitable areas in Arkansas,

Arizona, California, Colorado, Idaho, Utah, and Wyoming. Ngai (2005) writes about the incarceration of Japanese Americans: "The U.S. government never formally stripped Japanese Americans of their citizenship. But in effect it nullified their citizenship, exclusively on grounds of racial difference" (p. 175). The WRA set up additional segregated camps for Japanese nationals (classified as noncitizens) and US-born Japanese Americans deemed to be disloyal foreigners with nationalistic allegiances toward Japan.

Chang (2010) notes that a common "master narrative" about the World War II incarceration of Japanese Americans was that "the internment was justified as a wartime necessity" (p. 71). However, high school students, who are usually sympathetic to issues of fairness, quickly learn that the abrupt, costly, and poorly coordinated imprisonment of Japanese American families in the 1940s was wrought with multiple contradictions. More than two-thirds of those detained were American citizens by birthright, and more than one-half were children under the age of eighteen or people sixty-five and older (Ngai, 2005). More troubling, there was no evidence that Japanese Americans were disloyal to America or were engaging in acts of espionage (Weglyn, 1996).

Chaos erupted in the camps when the WRA administered a loyalty oath survey to all Japanese American detainees who were at least seventeen years of age. Two questions were particularly controversial. Question 27 asked if Japanese American draft-eligible men were willing to serve in the US armed forces. Question 28 asked respondents to swear unqualified allegiance to the United States, which included a section asking them to relinquish their loyalty to the Japanese emperor. Answering Yes-Yes meant that Japanese American young men would be fighting overseas in the name of democracy and freedom when their own families had none in their own country. Those who answered No-No for moral reasons would be deemed by many in their community as disloyal and unpatriotic traitors. Despite the outcry over the survey from many Japanese Americans, the Japanese American Citizens League passed a controversial resolution for all Japanese American draft-eligible men to volunteer for service. The all-Nisei 442nd Regimental Combat Team became the most highly decorated unit during World War II, but also suffered significant casualties.

Deep rifts opened up within the Japanese American community over whether Japanese American men should volunteer for service, further fracturing relations in an already fragile community. Known as the No-No Boys, Japanese American male dissenters were ostracized by the Japanese American community during and after the war for engaging in a controversial act of civil disobedience. Japanese Americans who contested the incarceration or whom the US government considered to be dangerous or disloyal were subsequently detained and segregated at Tule Lake, a high-security camp located in Northern California (Suzuki, 1986). The Renunciation Act of 1944 was created to encourage dissenting Japanese Americans to renounce their US citizenship, with the end goal of deporting them to Japan (Ngai, 2005). Many Japanese Americans who ended up renouncing their citizenship during World War II did so under anger, duress, or fear.

The Redress Movement: Partially Righting a Terrible Wrong

In the early 1970s through the late 1980s, Japanese American activists, including camp survivors, members of JACL, and political leaders across party lines, spearheaded what's commonly known as the Redress Movement, a coordinated community effort to fight for legislation to compensate living camp survivors for the significant emotional and material losses they experienced during World War II. After years of careful research and testimonies from camp survivors, the Redress Movement led to the passage of the Civil Liberties Act of 1988, which was signed by President Ronald W. Reagan. The act materialized into $20,000 reparations for each living camp survivor, along with a formal apology signed by President George H. W. Bush in 1990. While considered a victory by many, reparations couldn't by any means compensate for the full scope of losses that Japanese Americans experienced during World War II. The Commission on Wartime Relocation and Internment of Civilians (CWRIC) estimated that in 1983 dollars, Japanese Americans collectively lost upward of $2 billion in lost income and property, not to mention intangible damages, including the intense psychological suffering and trauma that camp survivors experienced during and after the war (Maki, Kitano, & Berthold, 1999).

Explanation of Common Terms and Pronunciation Guide

Commonly Used Terms

1. *Inu*—literally the Japanese word for "dog" but specifically used during World War II by many in the Japanese American community to refer to a fellow Japanese American, usually male, who was suspected of being an informant for the US government. In this context, an inu was seen as a sellout and a traitor.
2. *Issei*—a first-generation American or a Japanese immigrant.
3. *Nisei*—a second-generation Japanese American or the American-born child of Japanese immigrants.
4. *Kibei-Nisei*—a second-generation Japanese American born in the United States but educated and raised in Japan, returning to the United States as an adult. Often viewed by the community as culturally more Japanese than Japanese American.

5. *Sansei*—a third-generation Japanese American or the American-born grandchild of Japanese immigrants.
6. *Nikkei*—any person of Japanese ancestry outside of Japan regardless of generation or mixed-race status.

Names and Naming

In Japan and other East Asian cultures, it's common to see a person's name formally listed in the format of surname first and given name last. In Japanese American literature, especially when referencing Japanese immigrant authors or characters, authors may use traditional Japanese naming conventions. For example, in Jeanne Wakatsuki Houston's memoir, *Farewell to Manzanar,* the author's father, Ko Wakatsuki (given name is listed first in the Western context), is sometimes referenced in the film and text as Wakatsuki Ko (given name is listed last in the Japanese context).

Pronunciation

Japanese given names and surnames are relatively easy to pronounce once students master basic vowel phonemes, which are nearly identical to those in the Spanish language. There are only five vowel sounds in the Japanese language: a, i, u, e, o. As a language guide explains, these short vowels are "enunciated clearly and crisply," and gives the following example of an English language sentence to demonstrate the approximate sounds (Association for Japanese Language Teaching, 1996, p. 10):

A̱h, we̱ s̱oon ge̱t o̱ld
a   i   u   e   o

3 Jeanne Wakatsuki Houston's *Farewell to Manzanar*

■ ■

Though I was only seven, my images of certain people from this period are very precise.
—Jeanne Wakatsuki Houston, *Farewell to Manzanar*

Jeanne Wakatsuki Houston was born in Inglewood, California, on September 26, 1934. Her father, Ko Wakatsuki, was an Issei who arrived in Hawai'i in 1904 at the age of seventeen. Her mother, Riku Wakatsuki, was a Nisei born in Hawai'i and later raised on the US mainland. The youngest of ten children, Jeanne Wakatsuki was only seven years old when her family was incarcerated at the Manzanar Relocation Center, a US concentration camp built near the desert town of Independence, California. After the war, the American Friends Service Committee, a Quaker organization, helped the Wakatsuki family find a new home in a housing project in west Long Beach, California. The Wakatsukis then moved to San Jose, California, in 1952, the same year the Immigration and Nationality Act, also known as the McCarran-Walter Act, was passed, which allowed Japanese immigrants a pathway to become naturalized citizens. In prior years, US immigration laws prevented Japanese nationals from becoming naturalized citizens.

After high school, Jeanne Wakatsuki attended San Jose State College to study journalism and sociology; this was where she also met her future husband, James D. Houston. She earned her undergraduate degree, and a year later the couple married in 1956. Even though their home state of California officially banned antimiscegenation laws in 1948, negative attitudes toward interracial relationships were still prevalent when the couple married; these laws weren't completely banned in the United States until 1967. After college, Wakatsuki Houston had difficulty finding work because Asian Americans, especially Japanese American women, continued to face racial discrimination in the mainstream labor sector. In an interview, she shared, "I could not become a school teacher, and I couldn't even become a probation officer in the field, because, as my supervisor said, the community is not ready to have an oriental [sic] police officer" (Friedson, 1984, p. 68). Unfortunately, her experiences weren't unique; many other college-educated Japanese Americans faced racial discrimination when trying to find employment after World War II (Maki et al., 1999).

Wakatsuki Houston started to speak about her time at Manzanar only after her nephew asked about her experience when he learned about Japanese American history in a college sociology class. She didn't even share her experience with her husband until fifteen years into their marriage. In 1973, at age thirty-seven, Wakatsuki Houston released her memoir, *Farewell to Manzanar*, which she co-wrote with her husband. In the foreword, she writes, "It had taken me twenty-five years to reach the point where I could openly talk about Manzanar," and "writing [about my family's incarceration] has been a way of coming to terms with the impact these years have had on my entire life" (p. x). In a 1984 interview, her husband explained that talking about her childhood and writing the memoir was a process of healing, allowing her to reach:

> the point where she could say farewell to that, to the view of
> herself that went along with that, the sense of shame, the sense
> of humiliation, the deep-seated sense of low-self-esteem . . . all
> comes of having been imprisoned at the age she was, without
> understanding it, thrown into questioning her national identity,
> her personal identity—all ultimately reaching the point where
> she can say goodbye to that, and move on, out on her own
> personal evolutionary path, whatever that might be. (Friedson,
> 1984, p. 62)

Wakatsuki Houston's writing career flourished after the publication of FWTM. She coauthored *Don't Cry, It's Only Thunder* (1984), which details her coauthor Paul Hensler's work as an American soldier who helped foster mixed-race Vietnamese orphans fathered by American GIs. She wrote a series of autobiographical essays in *One Can Think about Life After the Fish Is in the Canoe: And Other Coastal Sketches beyond Manzanar: Views of Asian American Womanhood* (1985) with her husband. In 2003 she published her first full-length novel, *The Legend of Fire Horse Woman,* a work of historical fiction that traces the life of a Japanese mail-order bride from the time she arrives in the United States in the early 1900s to her incarceration in the 1940s. Wakatsuki Houston was honored with the Humanities Prize in 1976 and the prestigious Christopher Award during the same year. She also received the Woman of Achievement Award from the National Women's Political Caucus in 1979, and the Wonder Woman Award in 1984 for her contributions to social change (Fugita, 1999). In 2006 the Japanese American National Museum recognized Wakatsuki Houston with the Award for Excellence for her positive contributions to society (Discover Nikkei, n.d.).

FWTM has sold more than a million copies worldwide. While it wasn't written specifically for youth, Scales (2006) identifies

FWTM as one of the top fifteen classics of all times for young adults. Denshō similarly cites *FWTM* as a modern classic and memoir alongside titles such as *The Diary of Anne Frank* (Wakida, n.d.). Over the past three decades, *FWTM* has become more widely read in high school and university classrooms across the United States as part of units on American literature, ethnic literature, and the memoir. As Rayson (1987) notes, *FWTM* "is highly readable and at the same time does not hesitate to confront the cultural conflict at the root of every Japanese-American's experience during World War II" (p. 51).

Unique Features of *FWTM*

Set in the mid-1930s through the end of World War II, *FWTM* focuses primarily on the detainment of the Wakatsuki family and 10,000 other Japanese Americans at the Manzanar Relocation Center. Despite the gravity of their circumstances as prisoners of war, Wakatsuki Houston initially held a child's perspective on the events happening around her: "At seven I was too young to be insulted" (p. 31). But she vividly recalls key details about her family's experience from the time they left their home to the moment they were placed behind barbed wires such as: someone tying "a numbered tag to my collar and to the duffel bag" (p. 16) at the Greyhound station after the family was forced to leave home, as well as the physical layout of Manzanar, including the "twelve toilet bowls . . . arranged in six pairs, back to back, with no partitions" (p. 28).

As an adult, with the benefit of retrospection, Wakatsuki Houston was able to piece together the details of her family's traumatic past that she hadn't fully understood as a child. During their years at Manzanar, the author frequently saw her father become angry and violent. Not fully understanding his situation at the time, she initially viewed him as a bully and mentally unstable tyrant. As an adult, her view of him changed as she learned more about the historical details surrounding what her father and other Issei men had endured while detained at Fort Lincoln, a high-security detention facility in North Dakota. She came to realize that what drove him to violence and madness was the cumulative and traumatic effects of historical racism, which tore their family apart.

FWTM also provides readers with several important historical facts to situate the Wakatsuki family's experiences within a broader framework of the nation's political climate during the 1940s, especially in terms of the many racist and xenophobic anti-Asian laws that directly impacted Japanese immigrants and their descendants. The memoir opens with "A Chronology" that provides readers with a brief overview of Asian American history. When the US Congress granted naturalization rights to free Whites and people of African ancestry in 1870, it made no mention of Asian nationals. Until 1952, US naturalization laws specifically barred Japanese nationals from accessing the full array of basic rights available to other Americans, such as the right to a fair trial and the right to own property. High school students are often alert to the troubling parallels between the themes in FWTM and similarly nativist, racist, and xenophobic attitudes and policies that persist in twenty-first-century America.

Who's American?

At first, some students may be hesitant to read a memoir about a Japanese American woman who was born in the 1930s, assuming it's a work written by a foreigner whose experiences are dissimilar from their own. To challenge these assumptions, I post a photo of Wakatsuki Houston on a computer screen with the name "Jeanne

Wakatsuki" written in large block letters somewhere on a chalk-board or a whiteboard, and ask, "Do you think this person is an American writer?" Many students answer no or hesitate to provide a clear answer. When I ask for their feedback, they give answers such as "She doesn't *look* American" or "Her last name doesn't *sound* American." Such responses offer entry points to discuss the social construction of American identity.

I provide a brief overview of the author that reiterates the following central point: Wakatsuki Houston, who was born, raised, and schooled in California, is definitely an American. We also discuss the meaning of the perpetual foreigner stereotype (Tuan, 1998), or the common assumption that Asian Americans are foreigners rather than Americans. Having these conversations early on is essential to help students recognize that Wakatsuki Houston is an American writer whose experiences as a child and young adult have many parallels to their own lives. The author writes about several universal themes in *FWTM*, including dealing with peer pressure and questioning the various authority figures in her life. Many hands go up when I ask students, "How many of you've fought with a parent or older relative about topics like dating or marriage?" Students from immigrant and refugee families also find rich connections to the themes in *FWTM*, especially the challenges of growing up as bicultural Americans and dealing with societal pressures to assimilate to White American cultural norms.

Wakatsuki Houston has given several interviews that lucidly reiterate the American motto of *e pluribus unum*, or "out of many, one." I ask students to discuss their reaction to the following quote:

> Being "American" is not a question of race, tribe, or physical attributes. It is a non-physical identity—a state of mind that values freedom and governance by the people for the people.

> It values individuality, and hopefully will extend to cultural diversity, making the tapestry of varied cultures in American society a truly American value. Our differences are our strength and our power. ("Q&A with Author Jeanne Wakatsuki Houston," 2012, n.d.)

Rather than having students choose their own groups, I randomly assign them to share their responses in small groups to ensure that different perspectives are heard. The preceding quote suggests several critical points about the multicultural and multiethnic nature of American culture and identity. Following are sample responses from a group of ethnically and racially diverse tenth graders that highlight the range of their beliefs about what America is and who's an American. The variety of responses illustrate that students have different understandings of American identity depending on their own background and experiences.

1. Diversity is part of America and should be considered one of our nation's key values. But not everyone today is treated like an American. The burning of the Black churches and mosques shows that our society hasn't fully embraced diversity.
2. America should be a place where everyone and the differences we bring to this country are tolerated. However, there are a lot of divisions based on religion and race. Not everyone is willing to tolerate other people who are different from them.
3. While there is diversity in America, there's also an "American culture" that all people in this country should respect if they want to live here.
4. America does exist by our borders. We also have a constitution and a flag that symbolizes what our country stands for.

Note-Taking Guide

Since *FWTM* contains several major and minor characters, includes Japanese phrases or sayings, and covers many events and laws in the US context, I encourage students to develop a simple note-taking chart to help them keep track of characters, events, and historical details, as well as to pose their own critical questions. For instance, students might note that in Chapter 1 of *FWTM*, "What is Pearl Harbor?," the author's narration begins calmly, with beautiful descriptions of Long Beach, California, in 1941, and also offers a glimpse into her father's background. But the tone changes suddenly when she focuses on Japan's attack on Pearl Harbor.

Students can reference their notes later when they complete more extensive assignments or projects. Teachers have many options for student note-taking strategies: handwritten notes are still useful and easy, while electronic notes can be enhanced with apps such as Evernote and Google Keep. I've also had success with the triple-entry journal format, loosely based on the Cornell note-taking system. Figure 3.1 shows a sample template that teachers could reproduce for students by hand or electronically.

Chapter Number	Summary of Chapter	Questions and/or Reactions
1 "What is Pearl Harbor?"	The Wakatsuki family was devastated when Japan bombed Pearl Harbor. They burned and destroyed their family photos and other heirlooms because they didn't	Japanese nationals "looked exactly like the enemy" (p. 7), which had implications for Papa's American-born children because the US government racially profiled anyone who looked like "the enemy."

Continued on next page

Figure 3.1. Chapter note-taking guide.

Figure 3.1. Continued.

	want to be associated with the enemy (Japan.) The FBI detained and profiled Issei men like Papa because they were seen as dangerous enemy aliens.	Sample student response from an eleventh-grade student: *Much of Chapter 1 reminds me of the panic from the September 11 attacks. I'd see stories on the news about how many Muslims were targets of hate crimes because they "looked" like the enemy.*
2 Shikata Ga Nai		
3 A Different Kind of Sand		
4 A Common Master Plan		
5 Almost a Family		
6 Whatever He Did Had Flourish		
7 Fort Lincoln: An Interview		
8 Inu		
9 The Mess Hall Bells		
10 The Reservoir Shack: An Aside		

Continued on next page

Figure 3.1. Continued.

11 Yes Yes No No		
12 Manzanar, U.S.A.		
13 Outings, Explorations		
14 In the Firebreak		
15 Departures		
16 Free to Go		
17 It's All Starting Over		
18 Ka-ke, Near Hiroshima: April 1946		
19 Reentry		
20 A Double Impulse		
21 The Girl of My Dreams		
22 Ten Thousand Voices		

Character-Mapping Grid

Wakatsuki Houston writes about her own transition from a seven-year-old prisoner of war to a mildly rebellious teenager after World War II. At the end of *FWTM*, she reflects more deeply on her time at Manzanar and her pilgrimage back to the site as a young wife and mother. Other major and minor characters also undergo significant transformations over the course of the memoir. At times, it's challenging to keep track of all of the characters because the text doesn't present a linear progression of events. For example, we learn about Papa's childhood and journey to America in fragmented, nonchronological scenes. Wakatsuki Houston also sometimes shifts between the first-person and the third-person subjective viewpoint to reconstruct certain moments and scenes that she wasn't actually a part of. Chapter 7, "Fort Lincoln: An Interview," for example, is a reenactment of her father being interrogated by a government officer at Fort Lincoln. It's unclear whether she actually interviewed her father, interviewed other Issei men who were detained, or was putting together her best guess of what happened based on her own research.

What I've found is that character maps help students keep track of each character's evolution, as well as link related events, people, and places together to develop a more cohesive understanding of how the parts of *FWTM* relate to the whole. I usually wait until we've read approximately half of *FWTM* before we start to create character maps to ensure that students have enough information to start making inferences about each character's development. Figure 3.2 is a chart of the main characters I assign, along with assignment directions. Figure 3.3 is a sample character map for Papa. I ask teams to give short presentations, in which they briefly summarize key themes from their findings using some type of creative format such as a reenactment or a skit. For example, the team that presented on Papa produced a series of mini-reenactments. They started with reenacting the scene toward the end of *FWTM* in which Papa takes his family on the wild car ride outside of Manzanar. They then back-mapped a few other key events in his life that pieced together a more human portrait of his character, including the moment when he first met Mama, his detainment at Fort Lincoln, his arrival at Manzanar, and his argument with Jeanne about the way she dresses for the carnival queen contest at her high school.

Directions: I'll assign your team to further analyze a main character from *FWTM*. Your task is to map out your assigned character's evolution throughout *FWTM* on a poster "graffiti" board [a large poster is sufficient]or by using a freely available mind-mapping tool such as MindMup (www.mindmup.com). Use bullet points or incomplete sentences to summarize the information. You may also use relevant artwork, images, or symbols.

1. How does your character change, grow, and transform throughout *FWTM*? Give examples from the text, including a specific dialogue, moments, or scenes. Note corresponding page numbers in the margins to help you keep track of key details.
2. Discuss the benefits and limits of point of view when determining what information is known about the character.
3. Find 3–5 quotes from the text that support your analysis.

Figure 3.2. List of main characters in *Farewell to Manzanar* and activity directions.

Early Life	Before 1942	At Fort Lincoln	At Manzanar	After WWII
Born in 1887–a time of great political unrest in Japan after US Commodore Perry forced Japan to open its door to trade with the West. Came from an educated and elite family (samurai class) in Japan. Was very proud of his heritage. Was considered the black sheep of his family. Prepared for a career in the	Arrived to Hawai'i to find work; disappointed to see Asians were limited to working in sugarcane fields. Thought he was better than other Japanese immigrants. Worked in Idaho, Oregon, and then California in different jobs. Always seemed to struggle with finding steady work. Charming, handsome, popular, and a well-known man in the community. Loved to be	Arrested by FBI with no due process. Wrongfully accused by the FBI of spying for the Japanese government. Became a prisoner of war, and detained for nine months at Fort Lincoln before coming to Manzanar. Tried to maintain his dignity at Fort Lincoln.	Became an alcoholic. Showed signs of PTSD. Aged several years and had to use a cane; seen limping. Became angry and violent toward his family and others. At one point, threatens to kill Mama. Angry that his children were becoming too "American." Wants Jeanne to become more "Japanese" but fails because she wants to be 100% "American."	While leaving camp, goes on a wild car ride—his first breath of freedom. Symbolically castrated. Struggles to find work after the end of World War II. Mama becomes the breadwinner of the family. His children move to the East Coast. Others grow up/move away from family. He "loses" his children. Quits drinking.

Continued on next page

Figure 3.3. Sample character map for Wakatsuki Ko (Papa).

Figure 3.3. Continued.

| Japanese navy. Left Japan at age 17 to go to US. Family in Japan assumed he was dead for years. | the center of attention. Was seen as arrogant, contrarian, and hot-tempered. | | Called an inu or dog by other Japanese Americans in camp because they suspected that he "ratted out" other Issei. | |

Sample Salient Quotes:
"For all his boasts and high intentions, he never quite finished
    anything he set out to do" (p. 49).
"He was not a great man. He wasn't even a successful man. He was
    a poser, a braggart, and a tyrant. But he had held onto his self-
    respect, he dreamed grand dreams" (p. 53).
"[Papa and other Issei men] had no rights, no home, no control
    over [their] lives" (p. 65).

After each team presents, I invite the other students to ask questions or respond to one another using the graffiti board method, or to add their own comments and questions to each mindmap or poster with sticky notes. I capture the comments from all of the posters by having each group summarize the content in a Google Doc. We constantly refer to this document when discussing characterization, conflict between characters, and specific dialogues in *FWTM*.

Major Themes in *FWTM*

To prepare students for more extensive projects such as creating their own multimedia products or writing persuasive essays, research papers, or their own critical reviews, I provide a brief overview of a few of the emergent themes in *FWTM*: identity/race relations, depictions of trauma, and untold stories of riots and resistors. Wakatsuki Houston tends to describe various events, feelings, and people in binary terms, such as contrasting American versus Japanese culture or the old versus the young, which allows students to easily detect patterns in the text as they look for supporting evidence. Teachers could use these themes as a guide to direct students to explore specific events or topics in greater detail.

Identity and Race Relations

Frequent reference is made to the author's construction of American (White/desirable) versus foreign (Japanese/undesirable) cultures, identities, and people throughout the memoir. While focusing on some key elements of bicultural identity development is a helpful start for students who may not be familiar with theories of ethnic identity, I also challenge them to move beyond simplistic understandings of culture because too often, literary analyses of cultural identity in Asian American literature reinforce one-dimensional stereotypes such as that biculturalism solely defines all Asian American people's experiences, that White Americans are more socially desirable than Asian Americans, or both (Endo, 2009). Wakatsuki Houston herself internalized some of these messages as a child, as evidenced through her recollection that "[Papa] was unforgivably a foreigner then, foreigner to them [Whites], foreign to me, foreign to everyone but Mama" (p. 151).

Most secondary students are able to detect the salient representations of bicultural identity and intergenerational conflicts in

FWTM. Obvious examples include frequent reference to Japanese clothing, food, and language, as well as culturally based interactions between child and parent and between husband and wife that are often hierarchical due to factors such as age and gender. Contrasting immigrant family members to American-born ones is another juxtaposition strategy. For example, Granny and Papa, as Japanese nationals and "aliens" ineligible for American citizenship (p. 6), are frequently contrasted to their American-born children and grandchildren.

With some guidance, students are able to detect subtler aspects of cultural conflicts and identity formation in *FWTM*. Since the Wakatsuki family and other Japanese Americans were segregated from US society for three years while incarcerated, the foci on identity development and race relations after World War II enables students to draw inferences about the impact the incarceration had on the author as she transitions into young adulthood. As Wakatsuki Houston reflects on her reintegration back into a White-dominated society after the war, she writes, "They [White people] wouldn't see me, they would see the slant-eyed face, the Asian. This is what accounts, in part, for the entire evacuation. You cannot deport 110,000 people unless you have stopped seeing individuals" (p. 142). Consequently, as a teenager she attempted to remedy her perceived foreignness through contrasting coping strategies, living "with this double impulse: the urge to disappear and the desperate desire to be acceptable" (p. 143).

How various White American figures are situated in *FWTM* also offers opportunities for students to compare and contrast the timeless issue of race relations in the United States, as well as to engage with controversial topics that usually spark lively dialogue. However, most American high school students aren't familiar enough with sociological theories of race to draw accurate conclusions about some of these topics. Many secondary students in the United States are vaguely aware of what racism is, but many aren't familiar with some of the nuances, such as why Whiteness is an invisible yet powerful social construct in our society. Having them read and respond to Peggy McIntosh's 1989 classic "White Privilege: Unpacking the Invisible Knapsack" (different versions are available online) helps them identify specific examples of how Whiteness appears and reappears in *FWTM*, as well as in their everyday lives. Once students have the framework and language to analyze what Whiteness represents in American culture, history, and literature, they could further explicate the characterization of the Maryknoll nuns and Quakers, as well as minor characters such as Lois and Radine. Additional connections could be made to the author's own struggle with internalized oppression that led her to desire Whiteness and reject her identity as a Japanese American.

Students also appreciate how *FWTM* addresses several themes about identity and race relations that are still relevant today. Even though some progress has been made since the 1940s, most students are aware that not all Americans fully accept interracial relationships, and some may still view Asian Americans and other racialized groups as inferior to Whites. Moreover, many people of color today still grapple with issues of internalized oppression in a society that primarily values Eurocentric standards of beauty, femininity, and masculinity. Having students explicate the representations of interracial encounters and relationships in *FWTM* and asking them to make their own personal connections makes these issues relevant.

Sample critical discussion questions:

1. Describe the theme of daughter–father conflict in *FWTM*. Identify examples of specific conflicts that appear to have emerged due

to common adolescent–parent conflicts versus potential cultural differences between an immigrant father and his American-born daughter.

2. Explain how the author viewed her Japanese American identity as a child and then as a teenager. Give at least three different examples from the text to support your answer.

Individual versus Historical Trauma

Two types of human trauma are represented in *FWTM*: individual and historical or intergenerational trauma. According to the American Psychological Association, individual trauma occurs when someone has an emotional reaction to a negative event such as experiencing abuse, living through a natural disaster, or witnessing an act of violence ("Trauma," n.d.). Each individual responds differently to a traumatic event. Coping strategies could include attempts to forget the incident or to deny that all or parts of it occurred; having flashbacks or nightmares about the event; or experiencing longer-term psychological effects such as anxiety, depression, or posttraumatic stress disorder (PTSD). Historical trauma occurs when a specific group of people experience a significant injustice such as forced assimilation, genocide, mass incarceration, segregation, or violence that directly impacts both the survivors and their descendants (Michaels, 2010). Comparing and contrasting the depictions of individual versus historical trauma in *FWTM* helps students develop a conceptual framework for explicating the context and meaning of the Wakatsuki family's and other incarcerated Japanese American families' experiences during World War II.

In the Western context, trauma is often depicted as a linear process characterized by an individual's immediate reactions and outwardly expressed emotions following a traumatic event. In

FWTM the different types of traumas are depicted as complex, multidimensional, and unpredictable. For example, through the use of flashbacks from different points of view, Wakatsuki Houston weaves between the past and present to offer simple yet vivid descriptions of trauma's impact on her life, including the shifts that occurred from childhood, to young adulthood, to her adult life as a wife and mother. To help students organize the various trauma-specific incidents and scenes throughout the text, I have them look for specific quotes and scenes that fit the two definitions I've provided. I ask students to mark each passage they find as either "I" or "H" to differentiate between the types. If they detect evidence of both or overlap, they mark passages as "I/H." I first model this activity with the following quotes:

Quote/Page Number	I, H, or I/H	Comments
pp. 62–63—scene where Papa threatens to kill Mama	I	Jeanne and her siblings witness their father going into a violent fit of rage against their mother after he hears rumors that others at Manzanar believe he's an *inu*. Papa threatens to kill Mama.
"In such a narrowed world, in order to survive, you learn to contain your rage and your despair, and you try to re-create, as well as you can, your normality, some sense of things continuing" (p. 89).	H	The mundaneness of everyday busywork at Manzanar, such as cleaning, gardening, and tending to the mess hall, helped incarcerated Japanese Americans pass the time. It also appeared to have helped distract everyone from a depressing and uncertain situation.

We further analyze how different types of trauma impacted Japanese Americans after World War II through the scene of the author's pilgrimage back to Manzanar three decades later. Wakatsuki Houston offers several significant observations that we discuss in detail: "The closing of the camps, in the fall of 1945, only aggravated what had begun inside" (p. 33); the reflection that "the traces [memories of detainment] that remained," and how "that hollow ache" gradually diminished but never escaped her over the years (p. 177); and "Papa's life could end at a place like Manzanar. He didn't die there, but things finished for him there, whereas for me it was like a birthplace. The camp was where our lifelines intersected" (p. 43). While these quotes speak directly to the author's individual experiences with trauma, they also, by naming Manzanar, allude to a broader type of historical trauma experienced by the entire ethnic community.

Sample discussion questions:

1. Describe how Papa experienced trauma at Fort Lincoln, at Manzanar, as well as after the war ended. Provide specific examples from the text, including dialogue, events, or incidents to support your main points.
2. Using the concept of historical trauma, describe how life at Manzanar affected the cohesion and structure of Japanese American families. Give at least three examples from the text.

Untold Stories of Resistance and Riots
Most American history books don't mention Japanese American activists such as Mitsuye Endo, Gordon Hirabayashi, and Minoru Yasui who publicly challenged the US government for incarcerating them in the 1940s. We also rarely learn about the mobs and

riots that arose during the World War II incarceration because of the deep political divisions within the Japanese American community. In *FWTM*, Wakatsuki Houston tackles these topics with an ethnographic eye. After their reading, students are able to articulate various explanations for why the riots at Manzanar started, as well as analyze the different perspectives around controversial themes, including the ethical dilemmas that both draft resisters and the 442nd Regimental Combat Team experienced.

Sample critical questions:

1. Why did the loyalty oath create such deep conflicts among Japanese Americans? What would a No-No answer mean? What would a Yes-Yes answer mean? How would *you* personally respond if given the loyalty oath, and why?
2. Research the formation of the 442nd Regimental Combat Team (also known as the 442). What was its significance during and following World War II? Describe why tensions occurred between members of the 442 and the No-No Boys.

Analyzing Themes through Multilayered Timelines

Since *FWTM's* nonlinear structure jumps around a bit throughout each chapter, I've found success using a multilayered timeline activity that gives students a sample set of events to explore (see Figure 3.4). As with any timeline activity, students are better able to visually organize emergent themes in a linear way. But a multilayered timeline also helps students move beyond events and facts to explore why certain events happened, as well as to draw their own critical conclusions and questions based on the text.

Directions: On poster board, make a multilayered timeline on your assigned chapter or event. Each layer should focus on at least two key events, memories, and relationships. Be sure to give specific details and examples.

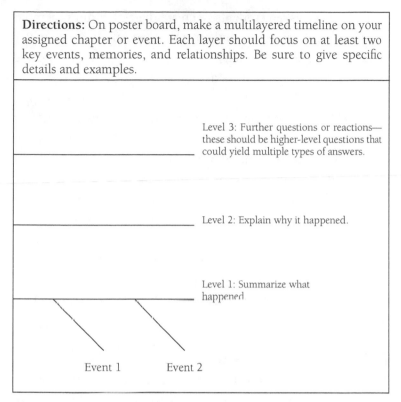

Level 3: Further questions or reactions—these should be higher-level questions that could yield multiple types of answers.

Level 2: Explain why it happened.

Level 1: Summarize what happened

Event 1   Event 2

Figure 3.4. Multilayered timeline.

Writing the Identity-Based Mini-Memoir: Inspiration from *FWTM*

I've also used *FWTM* to encourage students to write their own identity-based memoirs. Since writing a novel-length memoir would be impossible given the time constraints of the school year, in addition to adolescents' relatively limited experiences, I've found success in assigning mini-memoirs. Using the key themes raised in *FWTM*, I've asked students to create their own mini-memoirs that focus on some aspect of their various social identities, which could include class, disability, family, gender, heritage, language, nationality, race, religion, sexual orientation, and many others. Most students enjoy this activity because it allows them to apply what they've learned from *FWTM* to construct their own narratives.

As a caveat, writing about one's family history, issues of identity, or both, may be a painful process for some students. Students who are adopted, in foster care, or whose ancestors were colonized or enslaved may be missing key pieces of their family histories that aren't easily recoverable or traceable. Therefore, some flexibility is essential to allow students with different lived experiences to construct their own mini-memoirs in a way that's relevant to them and sensitive to their respective situations. Another option is for students to create mini-memoirs from the perspective of a major or minor character in *FWTM*.

Prereadings and Discussions

As a class, we write out the key traits of effective memoirs to ensure that everyone's on the same page. I use Kathryn Gullo's "Easing into Memoirs" (n.d.) guide for facilitating a conversation with students and eventually creating a rubric with them that includes key points about defining the essential characteristics of a memoir. The main elements we usually come up with include:

1. A memoir depicts an author's real-life experiences with a memorable event, person, or place. It's generally limited to a specific place, theme, or time.
2. It's written from the first-person viewpoint—uses *I, me, mine,* and *my.*

3. A memoir's intended to influence the reader to empathize (but not necessarily agree) with the author's experiences and perspectives.
4. Other details include developing authentic dialogue and complex characters, as well as using vivid language to help readers imagine themselves in each moment as if they were there during that particular place and time.

We discuss creating a structure that's organized and readable while challenging readers to mentally deconstruct certain conflicts or moral messages through specific strategies such as ambiguity or juxtaposition.

To get started, we read a short article by Abigail Thomas titled "How to Write Your Own Memoir" from *O, The Oprah Magazine* (2008): www.oprah.com/omagazine/How-to-Write-Your-Memoir-by-Abigail-Thomas. I also invite students to read five different youth-created memoirs from this list: http://teacher .scholastic.com/writeit/readwork.asp?Genre=Memoir. I ask them to list what they liked about each memoir they selected, areas for improvement, and strategies they could use when writing their own memoirs.

We spend some time discussing the specific features of *FWTM* compared to other memoirs. For example, *FWTM* doesn't follow a linear structure, occasionally uses bilingual prose, and vacillates between multiple perspectives and viewpoints. While most students have become accustomed to tracing a protagonist's major life events in chronological order, *FWTM* illustrates how trauma disrupts the structures of linear narratives and plotlines. We also discuss the ways in which Wakatsuki Houston's memoir illuminates memories of her relationships with others, as well as observations or reconstructions of events that she wasn't directly a part of.

Unlike most autobiographies and memoirs, in which authors write solely based on their own memories, *FWTM* is a carefully researched project that captures multiple perspectives in a larger attempt to educate readers about the untold history of all incarcerated Japanese Americans. The process started with Wakatsuki Houston tape-recording her childhood recollections, as well as consulting academic sources and interviewing other camp survivors, including her own family members, when she couldn't recall the details of specific events on her own (Moser, 2001). Although students can't invest the time that Wakatsuki Houston put into writing *FWTM*, I invite them to think about other ways they could collect information to use in their memoirs, such as interviewing family members or spending time thinking about an event and then recording or writing as many details as possible.

Students experiment with different literary devices that Wakatsuki Houston employs in *FWTM* such as figurative language, and figures of speech such as euphemism and oxymoron. For example, most students notice how Wakatsuki Houston uses descriptive language to help us imagine ourselves experiencing the harsh and uninhabitable conditions of Manzanar through descriptions of the "bitter cold" and "wind" (p. 20); "icy gusts of wind" and "fresh dust" (p. 23); as well as the frequent sandstorms (p. 79, p. 80). Students also note that the author writes about mundane events and random thoughts that don't necessarily grab their attention. Finally, while some students believe they need to write memorable memoirs, I remind them that a good memoir need not read like a thriller and may, like *FWTM,* contain uneventful details about a major event or experience.

The Politics of Memory and Remembering

Reading *FWTM* raises several questions about authenticity, human memory, and representation. To expect one person's memoir to represent an entire ethnic group's experiences or a major historic moment could be problematic, although teachers tend to fall into this trap because we just don't have enough time in the school year to intensely study even one historical event or person in great detail. There are also practical questions about how Wakatsuki Houston—or anyone—is able to recall such vivid details of their childhoods. Before they start to write their own mini-memoirs, I ask students to think about the various benefits and limitations of relying on memoirs as primary sources of information. To jump-start this discussion, I provide students with an informal homework assignment, asking them to come up with detailed answers to the following questions about their childhood:

1. List all of the addresses you've lived at from birth to today.
2. Provide the names of all the teachers you've had in your life, including the grade levels and subjects they taught.
3. In detail, describe one of your close childhood friends.
   a. When and where did you first meet this person? What was that person wearing? What were you wearing? What did your conversation sound like? What did you do together? Provide as many details as possible.
   b. If you're no longer in contact with this person, explain when and why your friendship ended.
4. What's your most vivid memory from childhood? Describe it in as many details as possible. Try to remember the date, location, and people involved.

I give students at most a few days to complete this task to allow them to contact family members or friends, and to try to recall and reflect on these prompts on their own. Indeed, such a seemingly simple task of recalling key childhood memories is challenging. To date, no student has been able to generate complete and detailed responses to these questions. Some students even comment, "This is way too much work," which helps them appreciate how time-consuming it is to put together a memoir like *FWTM*.

We delve into deeper questions about the flaws of human memory. Using the gallery walk format, I post the following questions on poster boards and ask students to write down their thoughts, which we use later as a reference for the mini-memoir assignment. Underneath each prompt or question are sample responses from a ninth-grade class:

1. How is an individual able to "remember" the details of a certain event?
   a. Reading it somewhere like in a newspaper or watching it on TV.
   b. Keeping and looking back at journals or diaries.
   c. Dreams or nightmares.
   d. Conversations with others who were there or who were directly or indirectly affected by the event.
   e. Mind triggers—thinking about people who were actually there.
2. What does one remember (or forget) from childhood, and why? Create a T-chart with the headings of **Forget** and **Remember** to organize your responses:

Forget	Remember
▪ Our birth into this world ▪ Most everything until ages three to five ▪ Details of daily life that are routine ▪ Events that are boring or irrelevant ▪ Things we want to forget, like being hurt or rejected	▪ Usually, events that are either very pleasant or very unpleasant ▪ Our best friends and worst enemies ▪ Being rejected or bullied ▪ Beautiful pictures and scenes; fun vacations or trips ▪ Really interesting stories

3. What factors might contribute to the flaws or limits of the human memory?

   a. Humans simply can't remember everything that's happened to them.

   b. Drug and alcohol abuse clouds how people view reality.

   c. Not getting enough sleep might impair a person's ability to think clearly.

   d. Being stressed out and not being able to remember everything.

   e. Being afraid to tell the truth.

   f. Peer pressure.

   g. Being self-interested. Holding back the truth so you won't get into trouble.

The question about how accurately Wakatsuki Houston is able to remember such precise details from her childhood is further complicated by the structure of *FWTM*. In each chapter, we aren't always certain when Wakatsuki Houston is recalling her own childhood memories, reconstructing the memories of others who no longer are living (like her father), or trying to piece together scenes from interviews and primary sources such as diaries and letters. Keeping all of these factors in mind, we're able to read *FWTM* and other memoirs with a more careful, critical, and sympathetic eye.

To help students gain practice writing their own mini-memoirs, we start by creating six-word memoirs. Six-Word Memoirs is a project established by *SMITH Magazine* in 2006 that has expanded to its cousin magazine, *SMITH Teens*. The project was started based on the urban legend that Ernest Hemingway was once challenged to write a memoir in six words, for which he supposedly wrote, "For sale: baby shoes, never worn" ("Six-Word Memoirs Can Say It All," 2008). Below are examples of some of my students' six-word memoirs:

1. Cheerleader by day. Insecure at night.
2. This Brown girl speaks her mind.
3. Life changed unexpectedly when dad died.
4. Born with Asperger's. And other gifts.
5. Black football player. Future Barack Obama.

These examples brilliantly capture the complexities of individual aspirations, identities, and lives. Students spend several more days writing their own mini-memoirs based on their six-word memoirs, although they aren't limited to crafting their stories around their initial topics. While some students incorrectly assume that writing about themselves will be an easy task and want to rush through the process, I require them to submit at least three revisions. I also build in time for peer review so that students can offer each other critical feedback on authenticity and readability.

Having students write their own identity-based mini-memoirs helps them think more critically about how their life experiences and social identities have influenced how they interact with others and view themselves. Through this process, many students are learning and writing about their ancestry for the first time, which allows them to recover incomplete but informative information about how they and/or their families came to the United States. Students learn more about the formation of their own belief systems and biases and, best outcome, are able to learn important life lessons they'll carry with them into adulthood. Like a young Jeanne Wakatsuki who grappled with issues of belonging and identity as a young teenager, they also experiment with different literary devices to express themselves and tell their own stories on their own terms.

Connections to Other Memoirs

Teachers might consider pairing *FWTM* with other memoirs, including works written by authors of color, that tackle similar themes of family, historical memory, and identity:

- **Maya Angelou:** *I Know Why the Caged Bird Sings* (1969). Themes— objectification of the female body; surviving racism and trauma; and use of figurative language and metaphor to describe one's cultural identity
- **Assata Shakur:** *Assata: An Autobiography* (1987). Themes—criminalization of Americans of color by the US government, particularly those who critique White supremacy; the intersections of gender and race in identity formation; and tense race relations with White Americans
- **Anne Frank:** *The Diary of a Young Girl* (1947). Themes—growing up in detainment; historical trauma; and young women negotiating intergenerational relationships as they come of age

- **Daisy Hernández:** *A Cup of Water under My Bed: A Memoir* (2015). Themes—growing up in an immigrant family with an alcoholic father; negotiating gender roles; and struggling to embrace one's bicultural identity in a society that values Whiteness
- **Barack Obama:** *Dreams from My Father: A Story of Race and Inheritance* (1995). Themes—coming to terms with one's ethnic and racial identity in a racialized society; grieving through the loss of loved ones; and negotiating identity intersections

Reading Other Japanese American Memoirs

The following memoirs authored by Japanese Americans could be comparatively analyzed or paired with *FWTM*. As a side note, most existing memoirs by Japanese Americans are written by women.

- **David Mura:** *Turning Japanese: Memoirs of a Sansei* (2005). Born in 1952, Mura, a Sansei, or the grandchild of Japanese immigrants, grew up in a Chicago suburb. For much of his young adulthood, he considered himself more American than Japanese. In 1984 he lived in Tokyo for a year, where he learned more about Japanese culture but also realized that he was an outsider in Japanese society. Mura's time in Japan also helped him realize that as an Asian American living in the United States, he experienced many forms of racial prejudice. As most memoirs by Japanese American authors are written by women, Mura's memoir offers a rare perspective. *Turning Japanese* also provides a perspective on Japanese American identity from someone born after World War II.
- **Miné Okubo:** *Citizen 13660* (1946). This stunning graphic memoir includes 189 of Okubo's original sketches of life in detainment, first at the Tanforan Assembly Center in California and then at the Topaz Relocation Center in Utah. Brief but descriptive and vivid text accompanies each drawing.

■ **Monica Itoi Sone:** *Nisei Daughter* (1953). Sone describes her experience growing up as a Nisei in Seattle during the 1920s and 1930s. Named Kazuko Monica at birth, the author recalls experiencing cultural conflict as a young Japanese American girl who didn't see herself as Japanese until President Roosevelt signed Executive Order 9066 in 1942. At this time, she learned that her family would be detained at the Minidoka War Relocation Center in Idaho because of their heritage and race. With the help of a friend, the author was eventually able to leave camp early, and resettled in Chicago to work for a dentist. A key feature of *Nisei Daughter* is Sone's relatively forgiving attitude toward her community's and family's incarceration during World War II.

4 Teaching *Farewell to Manzanar* on Screen

■ ■

I think the reason why there was so much at stake is because Farewell to Manzanar *is only one story, and yet there are thousands of stories, 120,000 stories. Regrettably, thirty-five years later, nothing as accurate has been shown to the American public.*

—Interview with Akemi Kikumura-Yano
(qtd. in Newman, 2012)

Three years after the release of Jeanne Wakatsuki Houston's memoir in 1976, a film version of *Farewell to Manzanar* premiered on NBC for public viewing. Produced and directed by award-winning filmmaker John Korty, *FWTM* the film also represents a powerful community project. Korty collaboratively wrote the teleplay with Wakatsuki Houston and her husband; he also regularly sought their input before and during the filming of this ambitious project. Although Universal Studios wasn't willing to release *FWTM* as a feature film, apparently because of budgetary constraints, Japanese American activists successfully advocated for its revival after the terrorist attacks on September 11, 2001, starting with grant-funded reproductions on VHS that were screened in several California public schools as part of the regular school curriculum (Bridegam & Shigekuni, 2015a). There also was a public screening of *FWTM* at the Japanese American National Museum in downtown Los Angeles in 2011, ten years after the terrorist attacks. Korty was in attendance and said, "That's why I went into film, because if you do something that's worthwhile, it doesn't disappear. Things really can last. . . . It's wonderful for me to realize that [the film is] still relevant" (Yamamoto, 2011, n.p). A DVD version is now available for purchase through the Japanese American National Museum's online store and includes the 109-minute film, a 32-minute documentary titled *Remembering Manzanar*, and a 10-minute interview with Wakatsuki Houston.

A unique feature of the film version of *FWTM* is that the main cast consists of all Japanese American actors, which is significant given the severe underrepresentation of Asian Americans in film and media. Dori Takeshita plays Jeanne as a child; Mitsu Yashima is Granny; Nobu McCarthy appears in dual roles as both Mama (Misa) and Jeanne as an adult when she revisits Manzanar; and Yuki Shimoda plays Papa (Ko). Other prominent Japanese American actors who served in major or minor roles include Noriyuki "Pat" Morita (best known for his role as Mr. Miyagi in the hit *Karate Kid* series) as Zenihiro; Seth Sakai as Takahashi; Frank Abe as Nishi; and Makoto "Mako" Iwamatsu as Fukimoto. Another unique aspect of the film is that many of the actors were deeply committed to filming this project because of their own experiences as camp survivors. Pat Morita and Yuki Shimoda, both Nisei and born a year apart, were incarcerated as young adults: Morita at Gila River (in Arizona) and Shimoda at Tule Lake (in California). Many of the extras in the film were also camp survivors.

The Filming of *FWTM*

Discover Nikkei, an arm of the Japanese American National Museum, published a three-part overview that describes the cast, filming process, and social impact of *FWTM* the film. Martha Bridegam and Laura Shigekuni, both attorneys for the law office of Laura Shigekuni & Associates based in San Francisco, coauthored the content. Students can quickly skim all three parts on their own to gain background information about the collective vision for creating *FWTM* the film.

1. Part 1: www.discovernikkei.org/en/journal/2015/5/19/farewell-to-manzanar-1/ (Bridegam & Shigekuni, 2015a)
2. Part 2: www.discovernikkei.org/en/journal/2015/5/20/farewell-to-manzanar-2/ (Bridegam & Shigekuni, 2015b)
3. Part 3: www.discovernikkei.org/en/journal/2015/5/21/farewell-to-manzanar-3 (Bridegam & Shigekuni, 2015c)

Structure of *FWTM* the Film

Whereas *FWTM* the book consists of seventeen chapters with distinct titles, the film version is divided into ten unnamed chapters that loosely correspond to the book's sequence of events. I find it useful to divide the screening into four days if possible: three days to watch the film in 27-minute increments, and one full day to watch the supplemental excerpts. This schedule allows time to debrief with students after each day's viewing. I also offer to show repeat screenings outside of the regular school day, as many students prefer to view the film more than once before they delve into deeper analysis of its content.

One critical detail to keep in mind is that in *FWTM* the film, many characters' names, including Wakatsuki Houston's siblings, were changed from the original text. Likewise, some details about certain individuals in the memoir were altered or omitted for the film, which might make it challenging for students to keep track of character development, plot, and point of view. To address some of these discrepancies, I ask students to create a simple table (see Figure 4.1) in which they fill out Column A as a prescreening activity. While they watch the film, students fill out Column B and jot down notes or questions in Column C. We use these points to later discuss why Korty might have modified or omitted some of the details from the original text and compare our findings to other book-to-film treatments such as Alice Walker's *The Color Purple*.

A Book Character	B Film Character	C Observations or Questions
Wakatsuki, Ko (Papa)	Wakatsuki Ko (Papa)	In the film, he's shown as a loving father and husband. In the book, the author expresses much harsher feelings toward him, generally describing Papa in extremely critical terms.
Granny	Granny	In the film, she passes away early, and her passing is indirectly attributed to the family breaking apart while at Manzanar. In the book, she's still alive as the war ends; there's no mention of her death.
Wakatsuki Riku (Mama)	Misa (Mama)	Mama is represented in near-identical terms in both the book and the film. The plate-breaking scene is represented well in both the book and the film.
Bill	Richard	In the film, Richard dies after serving in the 442nd. In the book, nothing's said about Bill serving in the military. In the film, Lois (the White nurse's aide) is Richard's love interest. In the book, Lois falls in love with another Japanese American man but not a Wakatsuki brother.

Figure 4.1. Book-to-film character comparison. *Continued on next page*

Figure 4.1. Continued.

Woody (eldest brother)	Teddy (eldest brother)	The eldest Wakatsuki son is more of a central character in the film than in the book. In the film, he's depicted as super-patriotic to America.
Eleanor (elder sister)	Alice (elder sister)	In the book, Eleanor is a minor character, and we don't learn much about her. In the film, Alice is a main character, although she's mostly seen dancing or singing rather than speaking.
Kiyo (elder brother)	Calvin (elder brother)	He's a minor character in both the book and the film. He's remembered in both the book and the film for saving Mama after Papa threatens to kill her.
Chizu (Woody's wife)	Chiyoko (Teddy's wife)	She's a minor character in both the book and the film.
Fred Tayama	Frank Nishi	In both the book and the film, this character is assaulted before the riot at Manzanar by Japanese American dissenters for siding with the US government.
Joe Kurihara	Joe Takahashi	In the book, he serves in the US army. In the film, he serves in the US navy. Both the book and the film depict him as an angry and radical critic of the US government.

FWTM on Screen: Benefits and Limitations

Shea and Wilchek (2005) note that there are several pedagogical benefits to integrating film versions of texts into the classroom. For one, for a memoir like *FWTM*, its film counterpart effectively reinforces key events, moments, scenes, and themes from the original text. A book-to-film analysis allows students to discuss the pros and cons of translating detailed textual representations into an audiovisual experience and, time permitting, may allow them space to creatively recreate or reenact certain moments or scenes that were altered or missing in the film. Through film, Korty was also able to re-create key literary devices that Wakatsuki Houston used in the original book, including bilingual dialogue, figurative language, irony, juxtaposition, and symbolism. Overall, the film provides a sympathetic portrait of the plight that incarcerated Japanese Americans experienced during World War II. It effectively conveys the somber message that camp life, in terms of both the poor physical conditions in Manzanar and the psychological trauma resulting from being detained, negatively impacted the community's cohesion and family dynamics.

However, any filmmaker who's been tasked with creating a film version of a book is confronted with a challenge: deciding which key details from the original text to include or omit. Korty's situation was particularly unique because of a limited budget and a relatively short amount of time to put the film together (thirty-six days total). Significantly, missing from *FWTM* the film are events described in three consecutive chapters near the end of the book: Chapter 19, "Reentry," Chapter 20, "A Double Impulse," and Chapter 21, "The Girl of My Dreams." The exclusion of these final chapters erases the Wakatsuki family's life after World War II, which, in the book, is a major struggle to reintegrate back into a hostile, White-dominated society after their release from Manzanar. Ultimately, by analyzing the benefits and limitations of *FWTM* the book versus the film, students can explore the artistic and cultural merits of both versions.

Prescreening Questions

Following the structure suggested by Shea and Wilchek (2005), I provide students with the following list of prescreening questions to help them focus on crucial moments in the film, and also to make well-informed predictions:

1. All of the main characters, even those who are bilingual, immigrants, or both, speak English very well and without a stereotypical Japanese accent. Why do you think the filmmaker used this approach?
2. Whose point of view seems most prominent throughout the film? What differences, if any, do you detect between the film and the original text?
3. In the film, Jeanne (as a child) says very little compared to the other characters. Why do you think the filmmaker used this strategy? Was it effective?
4. Which scene would you identify as the climax? Explain your answer by providing your insights on the foreshadowing techniques used in the film.

I also have students follow a note-taking guide to help them keep track of various scenes. Beforehand, I advise them that the purpose isn't to take detailed notes during the screening, which could distract them from enjoying the film and understanding its macro-level themes. Rather, after each chapter frame, I'll pause the DVD for a couple of minutes to allow everyone to write down a memorable dialogue, moments, or scenes, or to raise concerns or questions that we'll discuss after we review all of the assigned day's chapter frames. Then, we brainstorm ideas about what we should take notes on. Common responses include:

1. Our emotional responses to a certain character, dialogue, event, or scene
2. Any major discrepancies between the book and the film
3. Stylistic effects from the film that stand out
4. Repeating or significant images, motifs, and symbols
5. Moments that are confusing or difficult to understand

See Figure 4.2 for an example of a simple note-taking guide. At the end of this chapter, I've included a short description of how each frame starts to help teachers determine when to pause and restart the film.

Chapter Frame Number	Start Time	What Stood Out Questions/Responses
Chapter 1	00:01	
Chapter 2	00:07:53	
Chapter 3	00:17:35	
Chapter 4	00:27:32	
Chapter 5	00:35:04	
Chapter 6	00:44:16	
Chapter 7	01:00:24	
Chapter 8	01:15:19	
Chapter 9	01:28:20	
Chapter 10	01:36:30	

Figure 4.2. Note-taking guide.

Online Class Back Channels: Pause, Reflect, and Share

While the film version of *FWTM* effectively summarizes the key elements of the memoir, I pause after we view a segment or between chapters to allow students to process the audiovisual information. Using a freely available online platform such as TodaysMeet (https://todaysmeet.com/about/backchannel) is an efficient way to allow students to ask questions, share their responses, or start discussions with one another. If the film and the bonus features are viewed over the recommended four days, teachers could create back channels for each day's discussion to keep track of every student's participation and responses.

In addition to allowing individual students to post to class back channels, teachers could assign groups or pairs to briefly discuss their responses and report their findings to the rest of the class (see Figure 4.3). The link to the back channel could be posted on a screen (there's a "projector view" that zooms in to summarize the content) or translated into a scanable QR code. The value of back channeling is that it encourages participation from quieter students, as well as sets up an informal environment in which students can learn from one another. Teachers can quickly check for understanding and also archive transcripts from each back channel session to document conversations and ideas that could be retrieved for end-of-unit discussions.

Sample Prompt: We just watched the first 27 minutes of the film. Think about a particular moment or scene that stands out to you or that you might have questions about.

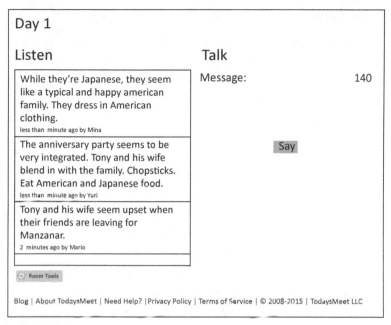

Figure 4.3. Sample back-channel conversation.

Whole-Film Analysis: Thematic Approaches

Korty and his team effectively highlight various themes from the memoir in the film version of *FWTM*. With audiovisual technology, the film emphasizes certain details such as the nuances of emotional encounters that would be more difficult to capture on the page. The following sections focus on major themes from the film that have some overlap with the book. Sample discussion prompts and questions are included under each heading.

Representations of Bicultural Identity

1. **Sample Discussion Prompt:** Both American and Japanese cultural motifs, scenes, and symbols appear throughout the film to highlight the Wakatsuki family's bicultural identity as Japanese Americans. Identify two examples, scenes, or themes that depict these types of bicultural representations.

Bicultural representations of American and Japanese cultures are prominent throughout the film through two tangible motifs: clothing and food. During the Wakatsuki's silver anniversary party, the theme of bicultural identity is represented through the display of food, including a mix of American (fruit and pig roast) and Japanese (sushi) dishes. All of the partygoers, including the Wakatsuki's White American friends, use chopsticks rather than forks. Clothing is another symbol of cultural and gendered expression. For most of the film, everyone, including Granny, Mama, and Papa, in addition to all of the children, wear formal Western-style clothing, including dresses, hats, and suits. However, at Manzanar, Granny is occasionally in Japanese clothing and eats Japanese food with chopsticks.

Code-switching is another representation of bicultural identity among Wakatsuki family members. In Chapter 2, we hear Granny or Mama mutter, "Shikata ga nai" (it can't be helped), and there are scenes when Richard and Teddy speak Japanese as bilingual translators. In Chapter 5, Papa translates the English language newspaper into Japanese for other Issei prisoners. English subtitles are used when two prisoners, speaking Japanese, claim that Papa is an informant for the American government and therefore a traitor. In Chapter 9, after news of the bombings of Hiroshima and Nagasaki are announced, Papa and the rest of the family sing the Japanese national anthem. One common trait shared by all of the characters is that regardless of whether they're immigrants or second-generation Americans, everyone speaks English without a stereotypical Japanese accent, a feature of the film teachers could highlight to prompt further discussion about how director Korty challenges the perpetual foreigner stereotype of Japanese Americans (Tuan, 1998) through both characterization and dialogue construction.

The film's musical selections include both American and Japanese classics. During the silver anniversary party in Chapter 2, Alice sings and tap-dances to a popular 1924 jazz song by Spencer Williams titled "Everybody Loves My Baby, but My Baby Don't Love Nobody but Me." Immediately thereafter, Chiyoko, Teddy's wife, is shown singing "Shina No Yoru" ("Night in China"), a 1938 song sung by a popular Japanese musician named Hamako Watanabe who was sent to Japan-occupied China to lift up Japanese troops. Near the end of the film, during Papa's speech in Block 16, Mr. Frizzell, Alice's music teacher, puts on a stunning bicultural musical performance. Alice sings the 1942 hit song by Gene de Paul titled "I'll Remember April" that appeared in the movie *Ride 'Em Cowboy*. After Alice's performance, a Japanese American male adult plays "Aka Tombo" ("Red Dragonfly") with the *shakuhachi* (Japanese end-blown flute). Toward the end of the film, Japanese Americans at Manzanar dance the jitterbug and watch American movies while also learning Japanese dance and songs. Because most students enjoy learning about music, I invite them to analyze song lyrics or the history of certain musicians whose songs appear in the film. Since most popular songs include timeless themes about friendship, love, and regret, I further encourage students to make thematic connections to other music, such as their favorite music videos or songs.

Juxtaposition through Symbolism and Words

1. **Sample Discussion Prompt:** Give an example of how the film-maker uses juxtaposition in dialogue, images, and words to make a moral or political statement.

I show the class a large picture of the American flag and ask students to share what this symbol means to them. Responses vary: American exceptionalism, citizenship, democracy, duty, fighting for freedom, land of the free, patriotism, and so forth. Interestingly, some students have responded by using descriptors such as capitalism, colonialism, empire, and protest. The variation in their responses affords rich opportunities to discuss how diverse Americans have had to grapple with conflicting messages about belonging, citizenship, and identity over several generations. We draw on the concepts of democracy and freedom to critically analyze how the film's juxtaposition of dialogue and imagery points out the ways in which the incarceration of Japanese Americans contradicted the all-American ideals and principles we'd identified earlier.

Characters in the film version of *FWTM* also make frequent reference to democracy, freedom, and justice, common connotations associated with America and key motifs, including the American flag and the Statue of Liberty. The American flag is a prominent symbol that appears throughout the film in different scenes. It's front and center at the entrance of Manzanar, a particularly ironic positioning. Korty also juxtaposes the American flag with symbolic contradictions of freedom, including concurrently displaying armed military police, barbed wire fences around the camp, guard towers, and the numbered tags that Japanese American detainees were forced to wear. Another example of a scene that effectively captures juxtaposition is in Chapter 2 of the film when Richard and Teddy enter an interrogation room as bilingual translators. Richard remarks, "It's wartime, Teddy. From here on, the Statue of Liberty looks the other way."

Moral Conflicts

1. **Sample Discussion Prompt:** The Japanese American community was deeply divided over how to respond to their situation at Manzanar. One side was highly critical of the US government. They believed that rioting was the only way to be heard and obtain justice. The other side believed that Japanese Americans needed to prove their patriotism by accepting their fate and having all Japanese American men volunteer for service. Decide which *FWTM* character's moral stance you most agree with. Provide examples of what the person believed and why, how other characters responded to her or him, and why you believe this individual took the right stance.

Deep community fractures based on moral conflicts is another centerpiece of *FWTM* the film. The complex dialogue is believable and emotionally engaging. The most salient moral conflict pertains to whether Japanese Americans should have been more critical of how the US government was treating them. The scenes in Chapter 6 depict the raw emotions of a deeply divided community leading up to the riot at Manzanar. Dramatic music and powerful visual effects such as the use of contrasting colors, still frames, and silence effectively reinforce the somber tone of the film around these challenging conflicts.

Students immediately pick up on how character juxtaposition is used to depict the dichotomy of pro-government versus anti-government ideologies. In one scene, Frank Nishi, the most pro-government character in the film, is severely beaten by a group of Japanese American men for claiming that the US government is protecting Japanese Americans by incarcerating them. In contrast, Sam Fukimoto and Joe Takahashi are deeply disaffected by their and other Japanese Americans' treatment at Manzanar. Throughout the film, Fukimoto and Takahashi are both depicted as angry radicals who incite the riot. I ask students to think carefully about which side they most agree with and why. Initially, students are conflicted in their views. While many see Nishi as someone who was ignorant and ill-informed but also doing what he thought was best given the circumstances, others sense that Fukimoto and Takahashi were taking an unpopular but necessary stance to protest the treatment of Japanese Americans and ultimately stand up to protest injustice in the name of genuine democracy.

Other *FWTM* characters articulate a less extreme version of this moral pro-government versus anti-government ideology dilemma. In Chapter 7, Papa and Joe Takahashi discuss their different stances on the infamous loyalty oath. Papa says, "It gives me a strange feeling to be suddenly sought out by the same government that denied me citizenship for thirty-five years." Joe agrees that the loyalty oath represents "the final insult" to Japanese Americans. But the two men disagree over strategy. Takahashi wants Papa to convince everyone at Manzanar to resist the loyalty oath, whereas Papa eventually answers Yes-Yes.

Making Comparisons: Book versus Film

As mentioned earlier, some key scenes from the *FWTM* memoir are omitted or rearranged in the film. Tapping into students' creative insights, I ask them to think about the pros and cons of how certain scenes are placed or reconstructed in the film. For example, the film opens with Wakatsuki Houston revisiting Manzanar with her husband and children nearly thirty years after the end of World War II. In the memoir, this scene appears toward the end of the book. Students often ponder the different effects of placing this scene at the beginning versus the end of the story. While some students prefer the book version because it has a more chronological flow, others like having that scene set the tone for the rest of the story.

While he left out some of the memoir's content from the final chapters, Korty added additional events to the film that weren't included in the book. For example, Granny dies in the film but not in the original *FWTM*. And while Bill in the memoir doesn't join the 442nd Regimental Combat Team, the film shows his counterpart, Richard, enlisting in the armed forces and subsequently dying in battle. Some students dislike the discrepancies between the book and the film because it's difficult to tell which events actually happened, but others believe that Korty added these scenes for both didactic and educational purposes.

Several new dialogues appear in the film that are rich for analysis and discussion. Since it would be difficult for students to identify and transcribe each new dialogue, I provide them with ready-made mind-map posters with each quote reproduced in large-size font. I ask them to determine how effective or not these additions are to the story, and what, if any, changes they would have made as the filmmaker.

1. Chapter 2: After learning from Teddy that the government might "evacuate" Japanese Americans from the West Coast, Chiyoko, his wife, says: "Maybe it'll be safer, Teddy. People hate us this much." Richard angrily asks why German Americans and Italian Americans aren't also being forcibly removed from their homes. Mama replies, "Look in the mirror, Richie. We can change our names, but we can never change our faces."

2. Chapter 3: On the bus ride to Manzanar, we hear from Joe Takahashi, the man in uniform. We learn that he was in the US Navy
   during World War I at the age of nineteen. He earned five stripes
   and several medals during his two years of service. He's shown
   saying, "They didn't care about my slant eyes then." When Teddy
   jokes that he "doesn't look American to me," Joe becomes angry
   and states that he's "just as American as that [White] bus driver."
   Becoming more agitated, Joe yells, "What's the matter with you
   people? Don't you realize what they're doing to us is outrageous?"
3. Chapter 5: The scene in a darkroom. Jeanne asks Mr. Zenihiro if
   taking pictures in camp is illegal. He notes that taking pictures is
   not only prohibited at Manzanar, but it's also against the law. He
   says, "One day when this is all over, a lot of people [will] want to
   forget it ever happened. But my pictures will not let them forget."
4. Chapter 6: At the block meeting, Joe Takahashi is being highly
   critical of the White American camp administrators. He demands
   bilingual meetings in English and Japanese to allow Japanese
   immigrants a voice in camp affairs. Someone suddenly turns off
   the lights, and Sam Fukimoto and his posse storm in. Fukimoto
   angrily states, "I'm through with the government. I'll tell you why.
   I've been a citizen of this country all my life. I used to love this
   country. I tried very hard to be a good American. But now I see
   that this country doesn't want me. It doesn't want any of us."
5. Chapter 7: Teddy wants to volunteer for the army, but Papa is
   against it. Teddy tells Papa, "America's at war; I'm an American
   citizen." Papa responds, "And I am not. They may not allow you
   to remain one. Look where they have put us!" When Teddy points
   out that he must volunteer because Papa is ineligible to as a Japanese national, we see tunnel-vision flashbacks of Papa experiencing symptoms of PTSD in Fort Lincoln. We then see him turn to

alcoholism at Manzanar, and then view his downward spiral into despondency and violence.

6. Chapter 9: Papa, who didn't attend Richard's funeral, is walking toward the fence to look outside of the camp. Joe Takahashi visits him to pay his respects. Papa says, "I no longer know what it feels like to be angry. I feel nothing. I'm dead too." Joe tries to remind Papa to be strong for his family and new grandson. Papa replies: "But I can no longer pretend. I have no control over my life or my family's lives. I wish I could go crazy . . . like this world."

Postscreening Questions

Following are sample discussion questions or essay prompts based on watching the film version of *FWTM*. Two accompanying examples of students' work illustrate how young adults are able to critically analyze aesthetics, characterization, dialogue, and form, as well as make impressive comparisons between the book and film versions of *FWTM*.

1. Describe the function and purpose of communication (including nonverbal communication) and language in the film. For instance, you might explore how factors such as age, gender, and generation influenced how the characters interacted with one another. You might analyze scenes in which characters code-switch between English and Japanese. Find at least three relevant examples from the film, including evidence of a character's development, dialogue between characters, and specific moments or scenes that stood out.

2. What key details or moments that you found to be most significant in *FWTM* the memoir were missing or not fully captured in the film version? Include at least two examples, and describe why you think these specific details should have been included.

3. Several binaries presented in the original text are directly or subtly included in the film through action, dialogue, and imagery/symbolism. Pay close attention to the contrasting themes listed below as you watch the film. Using a concept map, jot down examples from the film (e.g., chapter scenes, characters, conversations, images, symbols, etc.) that offer evidence of the following binaries. As you view the film, think about the broader message these binary pairs might represent.

   a. American versus Japanese culture
   b. Asian/Japanese people versus White people
   c. Calmness/stillness versus chaos and/or violence
   d. Freedom versus injustice
   e. Gender and gender roles—feminine versus masculine representations
   f. Collectivism (concern for the group) versus individualism (concern for the self)
   g. Old versus young people
   h. Papa's transformation before and during World War II (able-bodied to disabled, vibrant to depressed, young to old, etc.)

Sample Student Essay (Prompt 1)

Communication and language are two central features of both *FWTM* the book and its film counterpart. In the film, there are multiple scenes where English and Japanese [languages] are used including at Manzanar despite the fact that speaking in Japanese at the camps was banned for "safety" and "security" reasons. However, in the film, language goes beyond what's verbalized between people. The viewer must make inferences about the meanings of different forms of nonverbal communication such as silence. Ultimately, the film *FWTM* effectively conveys how communication and language functioned as means of freedom and/or survival for different generations of Japanese Americans during their incarceration.

In the Wakatsuki family, Granny really is the only person who appears to not speak English at all. In the film, she's basically silent, although we're able to gather some clues about her emotional state through nonverbal signals. At the beginning during the silver anniversary party, Granny is seen laughing and smiling with Tony, Papa's friend. At Manzanar, she primarily spends her days witnessing tensions boil over between different members of the family such as Alice and Mama, Mama and Papa, and Papa and his sons. The final moments when the viewer encounters Granny are literally in deadly silence: her funeral, and then in the final chapter where Jeanne visits Manzanar several decades later where the viewer sees Granny's cracked headstone.

While born in Japan, Papa is fully bilingual in both English and Japanese. Papa communicates in both English and Japanese with his family, although we mostly see him speaking in English in the film. When detained at Fort Lincoln, he writes to Mama in Japanese. Unlike the other Japanese immigrants in the film, Papa's dual use of these two languages allows him to navigate between the Japanese immigrant and mainstream White American communities. For instance, when around White Americans such as the interrogation officer, he easily converses in English. In Chapter 4, he translates a newspaper article from English to Japanese for the immigrant prisoners.

Another point to raise is that many of the main characters including the American-born Nisei are shown as speaking Japanese fluently. For example, Richard and Teddy were hired as bilingual translators during the beginning of the war. In Chapter 2, Teddy is seen asking an Issei prisoner a question in Japanese. During the block meetings, Sam Fukimoto and Joe Takahashi, the two Nisei men who strongly criticized the government for putting Japanese Americans in camps, are heard speaking in Japanese. Both also insisted on Japanese language use and translation at Manzanar to allow the elderly immigrants to have a voice in the community. While their ideologies differed at the individual level, many bilingual Nisei appeared to use Japanese as a means to show pride rather than shame in their heritage, and also, to help their immigrant elders survive.

Sample Student Essay (Prompt 2)

In the book FWTM, we learn about Woody's life-altering moment when he visits his aunt and other relatives in Japan in Chapter 18 "Ka-ke, Near Hiroshima: April 1946." However, any reference to this scene in the original book was outright omitted from the film. It should've been included because it shows how Woody, as a Japanese American soldier, came to terms with his Japanese American identity. It also gives context to the inner conflicts that young Japanese American men faced as they struggled to fit in either in America or Japan.

During his tour in Japan, Woody learns that his relatives thought that Papa had been dead for many years: "Your father was buried here in nineteen thirteen" (p. 128) but overall have fond memories of Ko. Woody also learns about the Wakatsuki family's elite lineage as a samurai-class family. All of these years, Woody and his siblings thought that Papa was a braggart. Through his time in Japan, he comes to better understand his father's experiences and learns more about his heritage.

This scene from the original *FWTM* also shows the hypocrisy of Executive Order 9066 and the World War II incarceration. Woody, an American citizen in his full military uniform, is in his father's motherland to fight for democracy and freedom. He must choose sides and must choose America. Woody and other Nisei men volunteered to serve in the US armed forces to prove that they were patriotic Americans. In Japan, we learn that "he dreads those looks [from Japanese people] that seem to call him traitor to his homeland or his race" (p. 130). At the same time, the film, through Richard's life and premature death, effectively reiterates some of these points, although it doesn't fully capture the resolution that Woody experienced when he was in Japan.

Writing a Critical Review of *FWTM*

Although the film version of *FWTM* has in general received a positive public reception, some criticisms from Asian American activists have been raised in terms of its cultural authenticity and historical accuracy. After its release in 1976, outspoken Chinese American author and literary critic Frank Chin (1976) wrote a scathing open letter to Korty in *Mother Jones* accusing the filmmaker of creating a "white racist vision of Japanese America" and misrepresenting "Japanese American history and culture" (p. 4) by altering the names of incarcerated Japanese Americans, and by not more directly addressing the extreme racism that Japanese Americans encountered before and during World War II. Another Japanese American activist, Raymond Okamura (1976b), also wrote an open letter in the same issue, stating that "you [Korty] have an obligation to insure that the production is historically accurate and representative of the broader Japanese American experience" (p. 5). Okamura ultimately contends that *FWTM* the film presents distorted, incomplete, and racist representations of Japanese Americans. In a follow-up review, he concludes:

> Farewell represents a skillful film-maker's utilization of drama, sentimentality, and nostalgia to distort an important lesson from American history. By distracting from hard issues and obscuring the root causes for the concentration camps, it succeeds in protecting, perpetuating, and promoting white racism. (Okamura, 1976a, p. 145).

I've had students read and respond to both Chin's and Okamura's critiques of the film because these men represent the views of Asian American activists who bring often-ignored perspectives to the table. Time permitting, students write their own critical reviews of the film version of *FWTM* to present in class that may affirm or contradict Chin's and Okamura's views. We read through the tips for writing film reviews in this short handout created by the Thompson Writing Program at Duke University ("Film Review," n.d.): https://twp.duke.edu/sites/twp.duke.edu/files/file-attachments/film-review-1.original.pdf. Since *FWTM* was created on a low budget, we focus less on cinematic quality and more on the elements of characterization, dialogue, motifs, sound, and symbolism, as well as comparing and contrasting it to the print memoir.

Brief Overview of Each Chapter in *FWTM* the Film

Here's a brief description of each chapter opening frame that will help teachers identify key moments and scenes, as well as plan for natural pausing points:

Chapter 1: starts at 00:01
A blue van drives down a long road in a desert-like area during daytime.

Chapter 2: starts at 00:07:53
In front of a fireplace, the Wakatsukis are burning family photos and heirlooms from Japan.

Chapter 3: starts at 00:17:35
Jeanne and Mama walk home from the grocery store and see a flier of Executive Order 9066.

Chapter 4: starts at 00:27:32
The scene opens on camp Manzanar at night.

Chapter 5: starts at 00:35:04
Papa and other Issei men are in a holding cell in Fort Lincoln.

Chapter 6: starts at 00:44:16
Sam Fukimoto is yelling.

Chapter 7: starts at 01:00:24
Weeks have gone by with no word from Papa. When word comes back that Papa is coming home for Christmas, the family is excited.

Chapter 8: starts at 01:15:19
A car is driving down a dirt road, passing a sign that reads: "IT TAKES 8 TONS OF FREIGHT TO K.O. 1 JAP."

Chapter 9: starts at 01:28:20
The camera angle provides the viewer with a perspective on the mountains through a chain-link fence.

Chapter 10: starts at 01:36:30

The scene opens with black-and-white photo of Alice and her high school classmates, the last graduating class of Manzanar High.

Film Supplements

The DVD version of the film, released in 2004, contains two supplements. One, a 22-minute documentary titled *Remembering Manzanar,* was released for public viewing and serves as an introductory film for visitors to the Manzanar National Historic Site. It incorporates government documents, historic images, personal photos, as well as voice-over narratives from camp survivors including Wakatsuki Houston. Depending on students' prior knowledge, teachers may want to show this documentary before screening the film version of *FWTM* to provide their students with a framework for understanding the historical context of the incarceration. Questions that teachers might provide students after viewing the documentary include:

1. Describe how and why Japanese immigrants came to the United States. What did they initially expect and hope for? Did they end up getting what they hoped for?
2. Why were the Japanese seen by many White Americans as "invading" America? What other immigrant groups in the twenty-first century are also accused of "invading" America? What are the key differences and similarities in how the first wave of Japanese immigrants and today's immigrant groups are represented?
3. The word *Jap* is used in this documentary in its historical context, but most Japanese Americans consider this word to be a hurtful racial slur, similar to the "N-word." What was your reaction to hearing the word *Jap*?

4. What surprised you the most after watching this documentary?

The other supplement includes a 10-minute interview with Wakatsuki Houston in which she explains how *FWTM* "is a human story." She offers insightful remarks about how her family's time at Manzanar and the treatment of Japanese Americans during World War II relate to current events because questions about racial inequities in our society persist. She also reminds us that Americans of different backgrounds share many of the same dreams, hopes, and personal struggles.

5 Lawson Fusao Inada's Poetry

The grandson of Japanese immigrants, Lawson Fusao Inada was born on May 26, 1938, in Fresno, California. His father, Fusaji Inada, was a dentist, and his mother, Masako Inada, was a schoolteacher. Inada was only four years old when his family was incarcerated during World War II. The Inada family was first detained at the Fresno County Fairgrounds and subsequently incarcerated at the Jerome Relocation Center in Arkansas and the Granada Relocation Center (also known as Camp Amache) in Colorado. After the war ended, the Inada family moved back to Fresno. As a teenager, Inada began to develop his identity as a person of color. At his racially diverse high school, he felt a close affinity with his African American and Mexican American peers and, as a result of these friendships, became interested in Black and Mexican American cultural influences in American literature and music ("Lawson Fusao Inada," n.d.). Inada also describes how meeting the legendary African American jazz vocalist Billie Holiday when he was eighteen ignited his interest in poetry: "Something was awakened in me. A spark. I was 18 and started writing poetry" (Brown, 2007, p. 1).

After attending Fresno State University, Inada earned his undergraduate degree at the University of Iowa; he went on to obtain his MFA at the University of Oregon (Wixon, n.d.). Inada initially wanted to become a musician but eventually settled on a career as a university professor, which allowed him to continue his community activism and poetry writing. Inada enjoyed a long career in academia as a faculty member at the University of New Hampshire from 1962 to 1965 before spending the rest of his career as an English professor at Southern Oregon University from 1966 to 2006 ("Southern Oregon Historical Society," n.d.).

Inada is the author of several collections, including *Before the War: Poems as They Happened* (1971); *Legends from Camp* (1993), which won an American Book Award; *In This Great Land of Freedom: The Japanese Pioneers of Oregon* (1993), coauthored with Akemi Kikumura, Mary Worthington, and Eiichiro Azuma; and *Drawing the Line* (1997), which received an Oregon Book Award for Poetry in 2000 (Sato, 2002). His edited collection *Only What We Could Carry: The Japanese American Internment Experience* (2000) is one of the most comprehensive accounts of the World War II incarceration, with a diverse range of primary and secondary sources, including government documents, excerpts from popular novels, letters, memoirs, and poems written by Japanese American camp survivors. Moreover, Inada is the recipient of multiple literary awards and recognitions, including a National Endowment for the Arts Poetry Fellowship in 1972 and 1985; Pushcart Prize in 1996; and Governor's Arts Award in 1997, and was named Oregon's poet laureate from 2006 to 2010 ("Southern Oregon Historical Society," n.d.). Inada has also narrated major documentaries about the World War II incarceration, including PBS's *Children of the Camps* (1999) and *Conscience and Constitution* (2004).

Inada frequently speaks about the core structural parallels between music and poetry. Indeed, people often analyze both poems and songs for metaphors, stylistic patterns, and significance to the human experience. Such connections are especially relevant for analyzing Inada's dynamic poems. The back cover of his collection *Legends from Camp* (1993) includes praise from critically acclaimed American Indian author Leslie Marmon Silko: "Inada celebrates b-bop and jazz; he sings love songs and laments from history, the Sand Creek Massacre and the imprisonment of American Japanese families only fifty years ago. Inada's ear for the musicality of English is unsurpassed." Inada skillfully incorporates musical elements into his poetry, writing with a distinct beat, flow, and rhythm. Many of his poems also celebrate ethnic music and pay homage to musicians of color. In *Legends from Camp,* under the section "Jazz," Inada titled several of his poems after famous African American musicians, including Louis Armstrong, Billie Holiday, and Lester Young. While Inada is most known for his poems about the World War II incarceration, his body of work demonstrates that his interests and passions extend beyond his ethnic identity and heritage.

Students are often intrigued by Inada's support for the idea of poetry therapy: "Beyond simply talking about issues such as loss, adversity, or childhood events, you've created something tangible. . . . I began writing as a self-therapy, a way of expressing myself" (Brown, 2007, p. 5). Inada also speaks about the importance of sharing poetry with others as part of the healing process, especially for people who've been traumatized. By learning more about Inada's purpose for writing poetry, students gain insight into the power of words, language, and storytelling. They also begin to think about ways they too might begin to use "poetry therapy" to express themselves—by writing their own poems.

In this 30-minute video interview, Lawson Fusao Inada reflects on how poetry enhances the human experience: www.youtube.com/watch?v=Eo-wPT6PlyA.

Poetry as Historical Recovery

As a young child in 1942, Inada likely had few tangible memories of his family's time in detainment. I share an excerpt from one of Inada's five-part poems, "Children of Camp" from his *Drawing the Line: Poems* (1997) collection, which he also performed with musician Pat Suzuki and actor George Takei. It offers a strong testament to the way that poetry became a part of everyday life in camp, and also illustrates Inada's use of personification; he likens poetry to children, families, and people, as well as to blood, dust, and mud (Park, 2015).

From "Children of Camp" (p. 115)

There was no poetry in camp.
Unless you can say
mud is poetry
unless you can say
dust is poetry
unless you can say
blood is poetry
unless you can say
injustice is poetry,
unless you can say
imprisonment is poetry.

There was no poetry in camp.
Unless you can say
families are poetry,
unless you can say
people are poetry.

Inada as a Revolutionary Activist

The white racists had to intern the Japanese Americans—120,213 of them—in concentration camps during World

War II. And they had to subject them to massive behavior modification and an indoctrination program to make them "Better Americans for a Greater America. (Chan, Chin, Inada, & Wong, 1991, p. xiii)

This quote is from Inada and three other famous Asian American authors, Jeffery Paul Chan, Frank Chin, and Shawn Wong, who authored *The Big AIIIEEEEE! An Anthology of Chinese American and Japanese American Literature* (1991), which is an expanded version of their original volume simply titled *Aiiieeeee!* (1974). These men are part of the first generation of Asian American activists who courageously made pointed and public critiques of White supremacy in US history, literature, and politics. In his own right, Inada has substantially contributed to the Asian American Movement, a relatively unknown part of US history that parallels the Black Power Movement and other social movements of the 1960s and 1970s. Watkins (2012) situates what she calls the "Power period" for African Americans and Asian Americans from roughly 1966 to 1981 (p. 114), although both communities have remained active over the past three decades because they continue to experience ongoing racial discrimination and exclusion in all sectors of life, including the criminal justice and education systems. The larger Asian American Movement grew out of demands made by the Third World Liberation Front in 1968 that led to the formation of Asian American studies and other ethnic studies programs throughout California and eventually in other parts of the nation (Espiritu, 1992). Gordon Lee's (2003) article "The Forgotten Revolution" from *Hyphen Magazine* offers a brief overview of the legacy of the Asian American Movement, which provides students with some background information to appreciate Inada's writings given his background and identity as a community activist.

During the mid-1970s, at the peak of the Asian American Movement, Inada and Frank Chin rediscovered a controversial semiautographical novel written by Japanese American author John Okada (now deceased) titled *No-No Boy* (1957) that inspired their lifelong efforts to raise public awareness about the untold stories of Japanese American dissenters and draft resistors during World War II. Initially rejected by the Japanese American community and other publishers because it portrayed Japanese American dissenters in a sympathetic light, *No-No Boy* now is considered a classic of Asian American literature. Inada wrote a foreword to *No-No* Boy's 1976 edition that included a tribute to Okada's courageous act of writing this story during an era when critical dissent was strongly discouraged by both White Americans and Japanese Americans. Inspired by Okada and others, Inada's poems about Japanese Americans have included paying tribute to "the Japanese community's outcasts, its 'no-no boys,' draft resisters and the vulnerable children among the prisoners" ("Lawson Fusao Inada," n.d.).

Some students, especially those who haven't learned about the history of multicultural America, may find some of Inada's works to be harshly worded or offensive. I start a conversation about Inada's contributions to ethnic studies and his political views to ensure that students have some context for his writings. I first project the quote referenced at the beginning of this section or distribute it on half-sheets of paper, then ask students to write down their immediate reactions, and then have them share their responses in small groups before we have a large-group discussion. Responses are usually mixed. While many students are surprised or upset by what they describe as the "angry tone" of the quote, others are intrigued and want to know more about the idea that the World War II incarceration of Japanese Americans was an intentionally racist political project. Whether or not students agree with Inada's views, providing them with a sociopolitical context for understanding his identity and social contributions to American literature as an Asian American activist offers a different lens for viewing his writings.

The following prereading questions can be used to synthesize the key points about Inada's political views and writings in relation to the key goals of the Asian American Movement:

1. Asian Americans are often stereotyped as apolitical, passive, and quiet. Based on the quote from *The Big AIIIEEEEE!*, describe how the authors have challenged these and other common stereotypes about Asian Americans generally and Japanese Americans specifically.

2. If the authors were in the room, what more would you want to know about their viewpoints? What questions would you ask?

Re/Writing History through Poetry

As a writer, Inada situates Japanese American poetry within an ethnic studies framework that seeks to educate his readers about often-omitted events, facts, and people in US history. For example, several of Inada's poems make compelling connections between the historical experiences of Japanese Americans and American Indians, especially within the context of his family's experience at Camp Amache, which, in a painful twist of history, was built on tribal land. As Burt (2010) writes, Inada "recasts the internment in relationship to US colonial projects that moved to dissolve, or 'terminate,' native communities in North America" while making comparisons between the "camp" and "reservation" metaphors (p. 113). Inada's poems also reflect on the consequences of historical missteps, including the centuries-long and systemic mistreatment of American Indians by the US government.

Since most high school students haven't taken courses in ethnic studies, they probably won't be familiar with certain cultural references in Inada's poems or the names of places that no longer exist. I start with the "Prologue" poem in Inada's *Legends from Camp* because it provides a readable introduction to the World War II incarceration. While this prose poem has some lines of verse, it also contains more extensive narrative stanzas that provide readers with important historical details. When passing out copies, I ask students to break up the poem into ten parts (numbered below) to help us keep track of the key stanzas and verses.

Below is a set of prereading directions to help guide students:

1. First, read the poem by yourself. If you don't understand a certain phrase or word, or if any passage is confusing to you, mark it with an *.
2. Once you're finished reading, jot down your initial reaction to the poem in a few sentences by reflecting on these questions:
    a. What main message do you think Inada is trying to convey?
    b. What did reading this poem make you think about?
    c. What characteristics or patterns did you notice in his writing style?
    d. What questions do you have for the author?
3. Highlight one line that stood out to you. Be prepared to share why you chose this line in terms of the emotions it evoked, what it made you think about, or what questions occurred to you.

Prologue (pp. 7–8)

(1)
It began as truth, as fact.
That is, at least the numbers, the statistics,
are there for verification:

(2)
10 camps, 7 states,
120,113 residents.

(3)
Still, figures can lie: people are born, die.
And as for the names of the places themselves,
these, too, were subject to change:
Denson or Jerome, Arkansas;
Gila or Canal, Arizona;
Tule Lake or Newell, California;
Amache or Granada, Colorado.

(4)
As was the War Relocation Authority
with its mention of "camps" or "centers" for:
Assembly,
Concentration,
Detention,
Evacuation,
Internment,
Relocation, —
Among others.

(5)
"Among others"—that's important also. Therefore, let's not
forget contractors, carpenters, plumbers, electricians and
architects, sewage engineers, energy, and transportation to
make the camps a success, including, of course, the administration, clerks, and families who not only swelled the popu-

lation but were there to make and keep things shipshape
according to D.C. directives and people deploying coffee
in the various offices of the WRA, overlooking, overseeing
rivers, city-scapes, bays, whereas in actual camp the troops—
excluding, of course, our aunts and uncles and sisters and
brothers and fathers and mothers serving stateside, in the
South Pacific, the European theater—pretty much had things
in order; finally, there were the grandparents, who since
the turn of the century, simply assumed they were living in
America "among others."

(6)
The situation, obviously, was rather confusing.
It obviously confused simple people
who had simply assumed they were friends, neighbors,
colleagues, partners, patients, customers, students,
teachers, of, not so much "aliens" or "non-aliens,"
but likewise simple, assuming people
who paid taxes as fellow citizens and populated
pews and desks and fields and places
of ordinary American society and commerce.

(7)
Rumors flew. Landed. What's next? Who's next?

(8)
And then, "just like that," it happened.
And then, "just like that," it was over.
Sun, moon, stars—they came and went.

(9)
And then, and then, things happened,
and as they ended they kept happening,
and as they happened they ended
and began again, happening, happening,
until the event, the experience, the history,
slowly began to lose its memory,
gradually drifting into a kind of fiction—

> (10)
> a "true story based on fact,"
> but nevertheless with "all the elements of fiction" —
> and then, and then, sun, moon, and stars,
> we come, we come to where we are:
> Legend.

Students notice that this free-verse poem doesn't follow a set structure. Each stanza is constructed differently; some consecutive lines have end rhymes while many don't. A large block of narrative prose is sandwiched near the middle of the poem that starts and ends with different connotations of the phrase "among others" (5), which also was used to end the prior stanza (4). Students also identify certain stylistic patterns such as repetition, which is used for dramatic effect. Inada starts several verses with "and," such as "And then" and "and as" (9); likewise, the lines "'just like that,' it happened / And then, 'just like that,' it was over" (8). Readers are left to grapple with how and why the experiences of Japanese Americans during World War II "slowly began to lose its memory, / gradually drifting into a kind of fiction."

Inada uses irony and juxtaposition to make a strong political statement about the incarceration as a major historical injustice. Eric, a tenth grader, effectively articulates how Inada employs irony to contrast the concept of historical fact versus fiction:

> In this poem, Inada uses irony to contrast the concepts of fact with fiction to make a point that historical facts aren't necessarily representative of truth. He starts the poem with "It began as truth, as fact / That is, at least the numbers, the statistics" (1) and then cites several facts about the incarceration of Japanese Americans including how many people were

sent off to the names of the camps. Yet, Inada challenge these various historical facts such as when he states that everything was "rather confusing" and "It obviously confused simple people" (6). In the last stanza, Inada uses juxtaposition when he alludes to a "true story based on fact," but nevertheless with "all the elements of fiction" (10).

Amelia, a twelfth grader, also offers a brilliant analysis of how readers who "read between the lines" will be able to identify juxtaposition:

Often, what's unstated in a poem is equally powerful as what's actually stated. Inada uses various forms of spoken and unspoken juxtaposition to critique how Japanese Americans were treated during World War II. Inada doesn't have to outright state that the American government was being hypocritical and racist. Instead, he uses juxtaposition to show that the government's decision was unethical and that Japanese Americans were more American than Japanese. In one line, he writes that it was not a matter of who was "aliens" or "non-aliens" (6) but rather how this historical event impacted all Americans and especially Japanese Americans. When he writes, "but likewise simple, assuming people / who paid taxes as fellow citizens and populated / pews and desks and fields and places / of ordinary American society and commerce" (6), the author reiterates that Japanese Americans are ordinary Americans. However, through what's not stated but inferred, the onus is placed on the reader to use this information to question why Japanese Americans were put into camps in the first place.

Connections to American Indian History

The poems "Healing Gila" from Inada's *Drawing the Line* (1997) and "At the Stronghold" from *Legends from Camp* (1993) powerfully illustrate how the incarceration of Japanese Americans intersected with the histories and lives of American Indians who had inhabited the land on which the camps were built. Prominent themes in both poems include an acknowledgment of the historical/intergenerational trauma caused by being displaced, forcibly assimilated, and relocated; Inada also describes the residual impact that institutional and societal racism have had on both groups. The timing of the publication of both collections in the 1990s is also significant. *Legends from Camp* was released shortly after the end of the Redress Movement that resulted in the US government's public apology and reparations to Japanese American camp survivors through the Civil Liberties Act of 1988 (Sato, 2002). This was also a critical time in American Indian history. The passages of the Native American Languages Act (1990), the Native American Graves Protection and Repatriation Act (1990), and the American Indian Religious Freedom Act amendments (1994) all speak to similar redress efforts for American Indians. In that same decade, both President George H. W. Bush and President William J. Clinton issued presidential proclamations to officially recognize National American Indian Heritage Month/Native American Heritage Month (in the early 1990s, President Bush also signed a bill that converted a weeklong celebration into an official Asian Pacific American Heritage month).

In the 1940s, the US government leased land from the Gila River Indian Reservation to incarcerate Japanese Americans at the Gila River War Relocation Center in Arizona. In addition to Gila, the government built a camp in Poston on the Colorado Indian

Reservation in southwest Arizona. This intersection between the histories and lives of American Indians and Japanese Americans provides an unusual opportunity for students to learn about comparative ethnic history and literature. Additional connections could be made between Inada's poems and the works of American Indian poets to contemporary social issues such as environmental justice and land rights. Since "Healing Gila" is a relatively short poem, we read it aloud together as a class, discuss our responses, highlight key stylistic features, and then engage in more extensive analysis of "At the Stronghold." Again, paragraph numbers have been added for easy citation.

Healing Gila
for The People
(pp. 110–11)

(1)
The people don't mention it much.
It goes without saying,
it stays without saying—

(2)
that concentration camp on their reservation

(3)
And they avoid that massive site
as they avoid contamination—

(4)
the massive void
punctuated by crusted nails,
punctured pipes, crumbled
failings of foundations . . .

(5)
What else is there to say?
This was a lush land once,
graced by a gifted people
gifted with the wisdom
of rivers, seasons, irrigation.

(6)
The waters went flowing
through a network of canals
in the delicate workings
of balances and health . . .

(7)
What else is there to say?

(8)
Then came the nation.
Then came the death.

(9)
Then came the desert.
Then came the camp.

(10)
But the desert is not deserted,
It goes without saying,
it stays without saying—

(11)
winds, spirits, tumbleweed, pain.

Here are sample discussion questions to provide students
after reading "Healing Gila":
1. Who do you think the author is speaking to? How do
   you know?
2. How would you describe the tone of this poem?

> 3. Analyze Inada's use of alliteration and anaphora.
> 4. Describe the possible meanings of the lines:
>   a. "What else is there to say?"
>   b. "It goes without saying, / it stays without saying?"

"At the Stronghold" is a longer poem that draws striking parallels between the cultures and histories of Modoc Indians and incarcerated Japanese Americans on land that, in 1942, was known as the Tule Lake Relocation Center ("Lawson Fusao Inada," n.d.). The Tule Lake site was located near a northern California city named Tulelake; it was also situated near the Oregon border. Kintpuash, also known as Captain Jack, was a chief of the Modoc tribe. During the Modoc War of 1872–1873, he led his band from the Klamath Reservation in Oregon back to their land in California. Captain Jack actively resisted the US Army's efforts to return the tribe to the reservation, but he was eventually charged with a war crime and executed by the army. Students are intrigued to learn that the title of this poem, "At the Stronghold," is named after Captain Jack's Stronghold, a Lava Beds National Monument in the North Sierra Cascades ("National Park Service," 2004).

The Tule Lake unit was one of the most controversial sites during World War II because it segregated Japanese Americans who were classified by the US government as dangerous, disloyal, and high-security threats. The National Park Service's website includes an excellent overview of Tule Lake that provides students with historical context for understanding some of the poem's references: www.nps.gov/tule/index.htm. I also ask students to read a brief biography about Captain Jack that includes information about the 1872 Battle of Lost River and the Modoc War of 1872–1873, available through the National Park Service's ebook: www.nps.gov/parkhistory/online_books/5views/5views1h11.htm.

"At the Stronghold" contains some names and references that may be unfamiliar to readers. Below is a short guide that teachers can distribute or go over with students in class:

1. Miles and Lowell (part of the poem's title): the names of Inada's two sons
2. K. Falls: Klamath Falls is a city in Oregon (p. 103)
3. Chinchinahtee (p. 108): refers to the city of Cincinnati, Ohio
4. Prisoner Rock (p. 110): refers to a landmark that separated Tule Lake and Coppeck Bay. Historical documents from 1946 show that American Indians had carved picture stories on the rock.

Given the length of the poem, teachers might assign specific passages for students to discuss in detail in small groups before sharing their analyses with the whole class. When class time permits only whole-class readings of certain excerpts, I offer the following two examples of specific parts of "At the Stronghold" that are rich with meaning, although teachers could select other passages by theme or topic:

Example 1 (p. 108)
"Question 27: Are you willing to serve in the armed forces of the United States, in combat duty, whenever ordered?"

No.

"Question 28: Will you swear unqualified allegiances to the United States of America and faithfully defend the United States from any and all attack by foreign or domestic forces and forswear any form of allegiance to the Japanese emperor, or any foreign government, power, or organization?"

No.

Hirohito?
Him people
like you na me.
Me no go
Chinchinahtee
Me go
Tule Lake
Me stay
Carifornia
Home

Students often debate why the narrator simply answers "No" to the loyalty oath. We situate the discussion within the historical context of why the Tule Lake site was created in the first place. The poem raises other complex dilemmas, including the reason why the narrator would rather go to Tule Lake than leave camp for "Chinchinahtee." Readers may also notice that Inada uses what appears to be broken or nonsensical English in the lines "like you na me / Me no go / Chinchinahtee / Me go / Tule Lake / Me stay / Carifornia/Home." A few students ask if these phrases are typos. I advise students that Inada didn't write these lines in error and ask them to look for clues about why he chose this strategy. I also have them look up the name Hirohito. Not all students know that Hirohito was the emperor of Japan from 1926 to 1989. Once they learn more about his life as a controversial figure, they're able to infer that the "No" response to Question 28 also alludes to the fact that Japanese Americans, as American citizens, wouldn't have had any reason to "form [an] allegiance to the Japanese emperor."

Example 2 (pp. 105, 110, and 112)
[p. 105]
Captain Jack,
I come to you

In respect,
Out of a need

For communion.

I will not dance and sing
In your sacred cinders

Where even today
The trail
Is difficult to walk upon.

We, too,
Walked upon this ground,
And through our
Stronghold
Was made for us,
To hold us in,

We, too,
Heard the geese in the wind,
The wind in the tules
And dreamed
In our brown bodies

Of peace and the good land,

Of home.

▨ ▨ ▨ ▨ ▨ ▨ ▨ ▨ ▨ ▨

[p. 110]
Captain Jack
Will be hanged
Tomorrow. "*Instructions*
To all persons
Of Japanese ancestry..."

[p. 112]
Captain Jack,
Father,
You teach us
To stand
To plant
Our feet in the ground
You teach us

To stand
To raise
Our eyes from the ground.

The following discussion questions ask students to think about the broader meanings of "At the Stronghold":

1. Based on what we now know about the Modoc tribe, describe the significance of Inada referencing Captain Jack in this poem.
2. Explain how Inada compares the cultures, experiences, and histories of incarcerated Japanese Americans at Tule Lake and members of the Modoc tribe.
3. What do you notice about how Inada writes about the earth, nature, and the environment in this poem? Find three lines from the poem to analyze and share.

Writing Poetry

I concur with Jago (2006) that "most students love to write poetry" (p. 8). Students of all backgrounds usually enjoy learning more about the hidden histories of various ethnic Americans or more about their own heritages through the medium of poetry. I have assigned students to write their own autobiographical or semiautobiographical Inada-inspired poems about a dimension of their identities, such as ancestry/history, culture, ethnicity, gender, race, religion, or sexual orientation. Another option is for students to write poems from the perspective of a Japanese American adult, child, or teenager who, like Inada, lived through the World War II incarceration.

I've also experimented with haiku, as well as the narrative and verse poems that Inada is more famous for. Haiku, a Japanese style of poetry, is an effective and efficient format for students to experiment with. In the traditional form, it consists of only three lines total, and uses the 5-7-5-syllable format for each line. Haiku is also usually characterized by some type of juxtaposition of ideas or imagery. However, many contemporary haiku poems, such as those published in Inada's (2000) collection by Japanese American camp survivors, don't follow the 5-7-5-syllable format. Rather, they retain the three-line length and the literary device of juxtaposition but use varying syllabic lengths in each line. Although not all Japanese American authors have written haiku poems, some poets have been able to creatively express emotions about complex topics using this form of poetry.

I encourage teachers to write their own poems and share them with their students. Students generally appreciate seeing us participate with them in the writing process, but they also learn more about who we are as people, with complex experiences. I share my identity haiku with students by silently showing them hand-drawn panes of each stanza decorated in large block letters with family pictures in the background:

This Asian American Speaks for Herself

Black hair/yellow skin,
Rejects assimilation,
For my ancestors.

The full directions for this assignment, found at the end of the chapter, involve students creating their own poems, sharing them in class through a three-minute presentation, and turning in a written reflection that allows them to share what they've learned about themselves as writers from this process. I allow great flexibility in how students present and share their poems. Students with musical gifts have played background music (including jazz songs by Inada's musical idols such as Billie Holiday and Bud Powell), or repurposed their poems into songs. Some students share their poems and reflections through spoken-word performances. Students with artistic talent have created background murals or handmade props. In a follow-up written essay, I ask students to make at least one major connection to Inada's poems or writing style.

After everyone in class has composed a haiku, we make time for a whole-class reading to honor Inada's belief that there's great benefit in sharing our poetry with others. Because some poems reveal deeply personal and sensitive information, before starting this activity, I ask students to quickly generate a few key community norms for how to respect the experiences of others during community sharing. For example, one person wrote about his fears of coming out as gay to his religious family, while another student wrote about her family's lingering fears of living in the United States as undocumented immigrants. One tenth-grade class came up with the following list of community norms:

1. Be present. Listen.
2. Avoid judging the person or making assumptions about them.
3. Keep sensitive information shared in this space confidential.
4. If you have follow-up questions, ask but be respectful.

Sixteen-year-old Elsa, the daughter of Mexican immigrants, wrote the following haiku.

I Am Proudly Both American and Mexican

Am I Mexican?
Or just an American?
Am I proudly both?

Elsa's poem powerfully summarizes key aspects of what many second-generation ethnic Americans are going through as they grapple with the multiple implications and meanings of their bicultural identities. Although the title is a declarative statement, Elsa ends her poem with a compelling question by switching the first two words of the title, thus creating ambiguity that's rich with interpretive possibilities. She also wrote her haiku as a series of questions, which she later explained was purposeful:

For many Mexicans [in the United States], it's hard for us to decide who we are. We're American but we're proud of our culture too. But can you be proud to be Mexican when the rest of America stereotypes you? Can you be proud to be just American when you're never treated that way? Reading Inada's poems reminded me of what it means to be Hispanic in American society. Like Japanese people, Mexicans have a long history in this country but we're usually treated like we don't belong here. Inada's poems also speak about Native American history, which is similar to Mexican American history. While most Americans think it's just a fun celebration, Cinco de Mayo has historical significance like with the Modoc War. It [Cinco de Mayo] was a victory for Mexico.

Julia, a White American student, wrote her haiku from the perspective of an unnamed Japanese American teenage girl:

Dangerous?

US Nisei girl,
The all-American girl,
Now the enemy?

Notice how Julia uses juxtaposition to show how the nameless all-American Nisei girl metaphorically becomes the "enemy." Like Elsa, Julia ends the last line with a question mark. In her presentation, she explained that she paired the words *US* and *Nisei* next to each other to show that they complement rather than contradict each other. Her word choices for the second line, "The all-American girl," were crafted to "show that ethnic Americans like Japanese Americans are actually just as American as anyone else, including European Americans." She ends her poem with a strong rhetorical question to "show how senseless it was to demonize an American citizen as 'the enemy' just because of that person's race." Julia, who particularly enjoyed reading Wakatsuki Houston's *Farewell to Manzanar*, explains how Inada's poems inspired her to craft her haiku from the perspective of a Japanese American teenager:

> While I couldn't relate to all of Jeanne's experience except for being a teen girl in America, reading her story made me sympathetic to her situation, which is why the main focus is on a Nisei girl like her. In my poem, I decided to title it "Dangerous?" to automatically suggest to the reader that they [sic] should

question the validity of the word itself. Reading Lawson Inada's poems helped me understand how poets can use irony to direct the reader's attention to an issue, problem, or question.

Connections to American Indian Literature

Because Inada makes frequent reference to American Indian cultures, histories, and legendary figures in his writings, teachers might consider pairing some of Inada's poems with the poetry of American Indian authors who write about themes similar to those in Inada's works:

- **Sherman Alexie** (Spokane/Coeur d'Alene): poems from *War Dances* (2009) such as "After Building the Lego *Star Wars* Ultimate Death Star," "Pow Wow Wow," and "Saturday Night Fever." Themes—historical injustice, historical/intergenerational trauma, identity conflict, and making sense of racial stereotypes
- **Shonto Begay** (Navajo): poems from *Navajo: Visions and Voices across the Mesa* (1995), including "Grandmother," "Darkness at Noon," and "Into the New World." Themes—embracing one's heritage, race relations/conflicts with White Americans, and resisting assimilation
- **Joseph Bruchac** (Abenaki): select poems from his website http://josephbruchac.com/, including "Crossing into West Germany" and "Walking." Bruchac has recorded his own readings of these poems rather than posting them in print, emphasizing the value of oral culture and storytelling over written poetry. Themes—ancestry/heritage, environmental justice, and motifs from nature

Other Japanese American Poems

There are hundreds of World War II–themed poems written by Japanese Americans that pair well with Inada's poetry. Many of the best poems I've found are also in Inada's edited collection *Only*

What We Could Carry: The Japanese American Internment Experience
(2000). This diverse collection includes poems by well-known
Japanese American poets and writers such as Shizue Iwatsuki,
Toyo Kazato, and Neiji Ozawa, as well as by anonymous camp
survivors. In addition, I enjoy using Chinese American Nellie
Wong's "Can't Tell," a short poem in *Only What We Could Carry*
about her family having to prove again and again to White Americans that they were Chinese, not Japanese, during World War II.
Wong's poem shows how her family's efforts were fruitless because
many White Americans couldn't tell the difference between the
two ethnic groups given the the racial stereotype that all Asians,
especially those of Chinese and Japanese ancestry, are the same.

I like to pair readings of Inada's poetry with that of at least
one Japanese American woman poet. Shizue Iwatsuki's untitled
poem below offers readers a glimpse of a Japanese American
mother taking her daughter back home after World War II ended.
While Inada's and Iwatsuki's styles are quite different, the didactic
purpose of their poetry is similar.

Untitled

Going home,
Feeling cheated,
Gripping my daughter's hand,
I tell her we're leaving
Without emotion.

Age, gender, and generational differences are also factors for
students to consider as they make inferences about the meanings
behind these different poems. For example, Iwatsuki was born
in Okayama, Japan, in 1896. More than four decades older than
Inada, she also writes from the perspective of an immigrant woman

who was in her late forties in 1942. By contrast, Inada, a Sansei born and raised in California, was only four years old when he was incarcerated.

Haiku Assignment

Assignment Part 1: Create a memorable haiku in the 5-7-5 format that either (a) speaks to some aspect of your social identity such as class, disability, culture/ethnicity, gender, language race, religion, sexual orientation, etc., or (b) is written from the perspective of a Japanese American who was incarcerated during World War II such as an adult, child, or dissenter. You'll share your haiku with the rest of the class in some creative format and also give a three-minute accompanying presentation in which you'll explain your writing process.

1. Your haiku should make creative use of at least one key characteristic of Inada's writing style that most appeals to you, such as alliteration, allusion, epanalepsis, figurative language, irony/juxtaposition, personification, or repetition.

2. Memorize your haiku so that when you present, you don't have to read it. Practice your reading multiple times to make sure that you enunciate each word and have just the right pacing.

3. For your presentation, share why you decided to focus on this perspective or topic. Be prepared to answer 1–2 questions from the audience.

Assignment Part 2: As a follow-up to Part 1, write about the significance of your haiku as it relates to key themes

---

we learned about from reading Inada's poetry. While there aren't rigid limits, I recommend a response that's around 2–3 pages long. Here are a couple of prompts to help you structure your essay:

1. Thinking back to what you shared, explain your reasoning for choosing the title and topic. Discuss any connections to your own experiences or personal inspirations.
2. Make at least one major connection between your poem and the poetry or writing style of Lawson Fusao Inada. Give concrete and detailed examples from Inada's works.

6 Hisaye Yamamoto's Short Stories

▪ ▪

The short stories of Hisaye Yamamoto are as subtle as they are blunt [. . .] she creates vivid images which prompt our imagination so that the reader is left to find his [or her] own truth.

—(Mylord, 2010, n.p.)

The daughter of Japanese immigrant farmers, Hisaye Yamamoto was born on August 23, 1921, in Redondo Beach, California. In 2011, at the age of eighty-nine, she passed away after experiencing complications from a stroke. While mostly having fond memories of her early childhood, she stated in an interview that her "adolescence was painful" (Cheung, 2000, p. 26), a statement that most American teenagers can relate to in terms of negotiating various familial, peer, and societal pressures. Yamamoto found her passion for the arts and writing when she enrolled at Compton Junior College to study literature and modern languages (McDonald & Newman, 1980). But at the age of twenty-one, Yamamoto's plans to finish college were interrupted when her family was incarcerated at the Poston War Relocation Center in Arizona. As Yamamoto recalls, "I was 21 when I was in camp, so I think I was pretty bitter because—well, you know, people say 'free, white, and 21.' I wasn't white [laughing], but at 21 people are supposed to make their own decisions" (Crow, 1987, p. 75). According to Denshō's entry on her life ("Hisaye Yamamoto," n.d.a), while incarcerated at Poston, Yamamoto experienced a tragic loss when her younger brother, Johnny, was killed in combat at the age of nineteen. Writing was thus a distraction that helped her to heal from her loss, as well as to pass the time.

After World War II, Yamamoto struggled to launch her writing career. Like other writers of color, Yamamoto experienced significant institutional barriers entering a field that was dominated by White authors and journalists. Yamamoto shares: "I never got published for many, many years; I just wrote for the Japanese newspapers" (Cheung, 2000, p. 29). From 1945 to 1948, Yamamoto found work as a journalist for a Black-run weekly newspaper *The Los Angeles Tribune*, which, in addition to promoting interracial friendship between African Americans and Japanese Americans, was the only newspaper in the Los Angeles area that had publicly opposed the incarceration of Japanese Americans at the start of World War II (Robinson, 2012). However, after running a story about a Black family that had been harassed by their White neighbors in Fontana, Yamamoto's life changed forever. A week later, the family was killed in what appeared to be an arson fire. Through her time at *The Los Angeles Tribune*, Yamamoto developed a heightened awareness of the blatant and widespread mistreatment experienced by African Americans in US society (Woo, 2011). Thirty years later, in 1985, Yamamoto penned a short story titled "A Fire in Fontana" based on the Fontana incident.

In 1948, Yamamoto broke ground when she wrote "The High-Heeled Shoes: A Memoir" for the *Partisan Review,* a short story that delved into then-taboo topics of rape and sexual harassment. In between raising her family and taking on various jobs, Yamamoto wrote occasional pieces for *The Rafu Shimpo,* a bilingual Japanese–English newspaper founded in 1903 in Los Angeles's Little Tokyo that's still in existence today. In 1986, Yamamoto received the American Book Award for Lifetime Achievement from the Before Columbus Foundation, and in 1989, her groundbreaking collection *Seventeen Syllables and Other Stories* (1988) won the Association for Asian American Studies Award for Literature. A revised and expanded version of *Seventeen Syllables* was published in 2001 with four additional stories. *Seventeen Syllables* now includes nineteen short stories that span Yamamoto's impressive forty-year writing career.

Yamamoto was a feminist and radical activist, unapologetically describing herself as an anarchist, antiwar activist, and pacifist (Cheung, 2000). As a young woman, she co-founded a local chapter of the Congress of Racial Equity in 1947 and organized protests against a public bathhouse that had denied Asian, Black, and Latinx people access to its services (Robinson, 2012). Yamamoto's short stories, which include a mix of historical fiction and memoir-inspired elements, have a unifying theme of centering Japanese American protagonists, usually young women, as imperfect people who, like all human beings, struggle to cope with personal failures and other life challenges.

Yamamoto is a literary legend, "one of the first Japanese American writers to gain national recognition after the war when anti-Japanese sentiment in the United States was still rampant" (Cheung, 1996, p. xi). As noted on the back cover of *Seventeen Syllables*, Booklist Publications likened Yamamoto to the critically acclaimed short-story writers Anton Chekhov, Katherine Mansfield, Flannery O'Connor, and Grace Paley, a comparison that was certainly unusual for an Asian American writer of Yamamoto's generation. Yamamoto wrote moving short stories about Japanese American history and identity, including intergenerational conflicts between immigrant parents and their second-generation children, interracial relationships, and the struggles that Japanese American women experienced in both ethnic and White-dominated communities. At the same time, she skillfully constructed complex characters, providing realistic portraits of flawed human beings who, like all of us, have regrets due to choices they've made around family, friendships, and intimate relationships.

Video Interview with Yamamoto

Denshō ("Hisaye Yamamoto," n.d.b) created a short video clip (http://encyclopedia.densho.org/sources/en-denshovh-yhisaye-01-0014-1/) of Yamamoto before her death that I like to share with students. Students notice that she appears to be a quiet, soft-spoken elderly woman, but they're usually surprised to learn that Yamamoto actually took radical political stances toward race and social justice. In this clip, Yamamoto reflects on the impact the incarceration had on the Japanese American community, which offers readers some context for understanding where she's coming from as a writer.

Sample postviewing discussion questions could include:

1. According to Yamamoto, how did the World War II incarceration impact Japanese Americans as a community?
2. What additional questions would you want to ask Yamamoto if she were still alive?

I also ask students to briefly respond to one of the following quotes from Yamamoto's interview, either as a quickwrite or through a think-pair-share:

1. "I think [the incarceration] is something we'll never get over, even with redress."
2. "That trauma has been handed down from generation to generation."

> 3. "We were found guilty without trial."
> 4. "There were sensitive people who killed themselves be-
>   cause of it" [the incarceration].

Elements of the Short Story in Yamamoto's Writings

The five elements of the short story—character development, setting, conflict, plot, and central theme—aren't always easily identifiable upon initial readings of Yamamoto's works. Rather, Yamamoto's stories "are layered in metaphor, imagery and irony" (Thalheimer, 1999, p. 178). American students are generally familiar with the short stories written by authors of European ancestry who tend to create linear plotlines with clear beginnings and endings, and who construct easily identifiable antagonists and protagonists. Stories written by women of color such as Yamamoto don't always fit within these traditional paradigms. I briefly explain to students that we should expect to do multiple readings of Yamamoto's short stories, which may still leave us with unanswered questions rather than clear-cut answers or conclusions.

Moreover, Yamamoto's short stories usually involve characters, dialogue, and plots that are ambiguous, complex, and nuanced. For instance, rather than depicting one specific setting, she often weaves back and forth between scenes before constructing images of fading scenery or memories of past places. Her stories also tend to depict multiple climaxes and conflicts that aren't easily predictable or foreshadowed. Having students document these multiple dimensions using multilayered timelines or writers' journals helps them see the relationships between key characters and events. The next sections detail the differentiated reading strategies I've used when teaching two of Yamamoto's more well-known short stories, "Death Rides the Rails to Poston" and "The Legend of Miss Sasagawara."

Reading "Death Rides the Rails to Poston"

"Death Rides the Rails to Poston" (1942/2001), thought to be the first short story written about the World War II incarceration, is a classic in Asian American literature. Yamamoto wrote this serialized murder mystery at the age of twenty-one while she was detained at Poston. First published in the camp's newspaper, *The Poston Chronicle*, this work of historical fiction is a somber portrait of how the early stages of detainment deeply traumatized Japanese Americans at both the collective and individual levels. Yamamoto also effectively draws our attention to human struggles that often remain taboo subjects in the classroom, such as alcoholism, mental illness, and suicide.

"Death Rides" details a series of events that occur as a community of Japanese Americans from Oceanview, California, board a train in preparation for their detainment at Poston. During the long train ride, three major events occur—the sudden death of an alcoholic passenger named Tsuyoshi Koike, whom "everyone hates" because he'd been an FBI informant; the poisoning of a young boy named Yoyo Nakamura; and what appears to be the murder-suicide of a young mother named Mrs. Kimi Ogata and her unborn son. The story's presumed protagonist, Shu Shingu, attempts to investigate the factors leading up to Koike's alleged murder, but through the process, finds himself unable to tell fact from fiction. Interestingly, most of the major events in "Death Rides" aren't certain, and readers are left to draw their own conclusions about whether the protagonist's account of the events leading up to Koike's death is accurate.

"Death Rides" contains multiple characters, conflicts, settings, and themes that mesmerize readers through prolonged suspense. A particularly unique trait of this short story is Yamamoto's construction of multiple climaxes: she doesn't use common foreshadowing techniques such as signposts to help readers prepare for the sudden and tragic events that occur. For example, the deaths of Koike and Mrs. Ogata occur suddenly without any forewarnings. A few readings of "Death Rides" are usually necessary to help students gather a more comprehensive portrait of how the elements of the short story appear in this work in predictable and unpredictable ways.

Character Grid

"Death Rides" includes several major and minor characters. Most characters have Japanese names that may be unfamiliar to most American students. To help them keep track of the key characters, I provide a character grid that can be referenced later when they analyze specific characters, moral themes, or scenes (see Figure 6.1). I encourage them to jot down key points and questions that

Shu Shingu—third-person limited narrator (also the main character and protagonist)		
Character	Summary	Questions
Tsuyoshi Koike	The man "everyone hates" who is suddenly murdered on the train.	Who really killed him?
Mrs. Kimi Ogata		
Yoyo Nakamura		
Toro Nogawa		
Pat Mori		
Mrs. Koike (Tsuyoshi's mother)		
Doctor		

Figure 6.1. Character grid.

may arise as they complete their initial read rather than focus on providing detailed summaries. After their initial scan of "Death Rides," I ask students to compare and discuss their character grids in pairs or small groups. I then summarize key points on the board to make sure that all ideas are documented, which helps students hear the range of questions that come up during their initial readings.

Analyzing Point of View

Yamamoto presents point of view in unpredictable ways. I ask students to come up with critiques of or questions about the limits of point of view, especially since this story is narrated in the third person from the perspective of Shingu, the main character. Following are sample questions or thoughts that a group of twelfth graders came up with after their first reading of the story:

1. Why do you think Shingu outright accuses everyone on the train of murdering Koike?
2. Did Shingu actually kill Koike? And/or did he kill Mrs. Ogata?
3. Did Mrs. Ogata really commit suicide?
4. Is Pat Mori a reliable source?
5. Why did Pat not tell Shingu about the murder she witnessed until after Mrs. Ogata commits suicide?

Based on the questions they generate, students could expand their analyses into more detailed close readings of the text. For example, Dara, a twelfth grader, provides the interesting counterpoint that Shingu doesn't seem worthy of being labeled the story's protagonist:

> At first glance, it appears that Shu Shingu is the story's main protagonist of "Death Rides the Rails to Poston" because he's

the third-person narrator. However, his unpredictable behavior throughout the story suggests that he may actually be more of the antagonist. One key issue that raises questions about Shingu's credibility is when he keeps accusing people on the train of murdering Koike. Directly accusing others of a crime without substantiating such claims with concrete evidence suggests that someone might have something to hide such as their own guilt. When he asks himself if he killed Koike and then vehemently denied doing so (p. 135), one is left to wonder whether or not Shingu's memory had its own limitations. Yamamoto's strategy to present his internal dialogue from the third-person limited standpoint is similar to the ways by which some murderers try to convince others, as well as themselves, that they really had nothing to do with a suspected crime.

Dialogue throughout "Death Rides" effectively demonstrates multiple limited points of view. Analyzing and making inferences from various conversations between characters will help students think about the limits of human memory, especially as it affects a witness's reliability in reconstructing a crime scene. More specifically, "Death Rides" gives students ample opportunity to analyze the credibility of different witnesses who directly or indirectly witnessed the same crime, and to consider the implications of relying primarily on witness testimony in the absence of concrete evidence and facts.

Teachers who want their students to engage in a closer reading of specific scenes could assign brief, 150-word responses that could eventually be expanded into more developed essays. I've asked students to use their imaginations to generate alternative possibilities to the main protagonist of "Death Rides" by analyzing the development of another character. Following is a sample assignment that asks students to argue that "Death Rides" has another protagonist besides Shingu.

> **Writing Assignment:** Pick a major or minor character of your choice other than Shu Shingu. Think of a character who might represent a believable alternative protagonist in "Death Rides the Rails to Poston." Write an argument for why that person could be seen as the story's protagonist. For your initial analysis, please limit your response to 150 words.

Here are some student responses:

1. Kimi Ogata is the story's real protagonist. While the story presents her as committing suicide and tragically killing her unborn baby, it's obvious that the incarceration took a major toll on her well-being as noted in the lines, "And the condition she was in, the hurried process of evacuation, the oppressing heat—everything combined in such a way that she was unable to stand it any longer, and her mind, already swamped with worry about her husband and the coming baby, cracked under the strain" (p. 140).

2. Everyone supposedly hated Tsuyoshi Koike because he was an FBI informant who ruined the lives of other Japanese Americans by reporting his neighbors to law enforcement. However, he could be seen as a semi-protagonist. When questioned by Shingu, Koike's own mother states this about her son: "He was always weak, not so much physically as morally. He was only doing what he thought was right, the best way he knew" (p. 136). Thus, Koike may have represented one of the story's protagonist[s] because he, despite his limitations, tried to do what was right based on what he knew was best at the time.

Analyzing Dialogue

Another intriguing aspect of "Death Rides" is the dialogue between characters. Each conversation between characters could be used as the basis to analyze larger themes such as how a community responds to a "snitch" to whether suicide is preventable. Below are sample dialogues from "Death Rides" that are ripe for analysis. Assigning small groups to analyze and discuss each dialogue is an effective way to jigsaw the content within one class period. Time permitting, groups could brainstorm ways to respond to the original dialogue they were assigned using another major or minor character's point of view, with the rule that they should closely emulate Yamamoto's unique writing style. Students also enjoy reenacting their revised dialogue, with some time to debrief about their rationale for choosing the approach, tone, and topic.

Dialogue 1: Shu Shingu's Internal Dialogue (p. 135)

"Did you kill the man, Shu Shingu?" he asked himself.

"Nope, he answered."

"I didn't think you did. But you're really sure?"

"Of course. Don't be so persistent."

"All right, then, you're eliminated."

"Thank God."

▪ ▪ ▪ ▪ ▪ ▪ ▪ ▪ ▪ ▪

Dialogue 2: Shu Shingu's Dialogue with Toro Nogawa (pp. 135–36)

"How did you feel toward Koike?"

"I hated his guts."

"You admit that? Why did you kill him?"

The young man was calm. "I didn't. He died of a heart attack. You heard the doctor say that yourself. He wasn't worth killing anyway. You don't know what that guy did. He used his new position to get petty vengeance on everyone

---

for every real and imagined slight. He tried to convince the government men that everyone he held a personal grudge against was a saboteur-potential. They caught on to him and kicked him out and promised that the ones who had been sent to concentration camps because of him would get the first hearings. If someone killed him, more power to that someone. Leave him alone, he's a hero."

Dialogue 3: Shu Shingu's Dialogue with Mrs. Koike (pp. 136–37)

"Do you hate your son?"

"Hate him? How could I? I'm his mother. I bore him, brought him up, watched him take his first steps, heard him speak his first words. Can any mother hate her son for remembering him in childhood, no matter what a rotter he turned out to be?"

She was cruel. He felt he had to be. "Let's not get sentimental. The child Tsuyoshi was an absolutely different person from the man Koike who betrayed his friends for trivial, personal reasons. Did you still love him when he lied to the FBI?"

"He was always weak, not so much physically as morally. He was only doing what he thought right, the best way he knew."

"Your conscience let you accept them?"

"He loved me. It was the only way he had of showing it."

"You mean hitting you?"

> **Dialogue 4: Shu Shingu's Dialogue with Pat Mori (pp. 130–31)**
>
> "You're a cold-blooded number, aren't you? If you knew all about it, why didn't you speak up? She needn't have killed herself or tried to poison Yoyo."
>
> Pat's face whitened. She began to cry quietly with huge tears rolling down her cheeks and making wet, shiny splotches on *Man's Hope*.
>
> "Why?" Shu insisted more gently.
>
> She shook her head. Her hands clutched tightly at the armrests of her seat. "I wasn't sure and I was afraid."

Exploring Point of View through Student-Created Storyboards
Having students create their own storyboards (either individually or in small groups) is another way to encourage them to explore certain characters, scenes, and themes in "Death Rides" in greater depth. While many students enjoy drawing their own sketches, others who are more self-conscious about their artistic abilities could use a platform like StoryboardThat (www.storyboardthat .com/), a free, web-based storyboard program that includes a variety of features, including the ability to add background scenes, callout text, and characters. This program also allows users to export the content into a PowerPoint slide show that could be shared as a formal presentation.

A storyboard assignment I've used asks students to investigate the point of view of another major or minor character in "Death Rides" whose perspective wasn't fully captured in the original story. Students can either share their storyboards in small groups or with the whole group depending on the class size.

> **Writing Assignment:** Create your own storyboard that pres-
> ents the point of view of another major or minor character in
> "Death Rides the Rails to Poston." You may hand-draw your
> own storyboard or use a program like Storyboard That. To
> start, highlight or underline moments and scenes throughout
> the story when your character is mentioned or speaks. In
> the margins, take notes about the character's demeanor, and
> write down questions that come up as you read.
>
> Below are the guidelines for your final product:
>
> 1. Include 3–6 storyboard panes. When you design and
>   format your storyboard, include appropriate and relevant
>   color schemes, images/pictures, and text.
> 2. In the dialogue callouts, narrate the character's point of
>   view using whichever perspective makes the most sense to
>   you. Be sure to create dialogue and situations that mimic
>   Yamamoto's writing style.
> 3. You'll give a five-minute presentation in class. Plan to
>   share your storyboard, as well as highlight key connec-
>   tions that you see to moral issues your character's point
>   of view might reveal. Be prepared to answer a couple of
>   questions from the audience.

Denny, a twelfth grader, created a storyboard scene (see Figure
6.2) from the perspective of Tsuyoshi Koike, the much-hated man
who was allegedly murdered during the train ride to Poston. Recall
that according to the Shu Shingu, everyone hated Koike because
he was supposedly an FBI informant who betrayed the Japanese
American community for his own self-interest. The storyboard
panes, which are based on first-person narration from Koike's
point of view, read as follows:

1. I was pressured by the FBI to share information about other Japanese Americans.
2. In the long run, what I told the FBI didn't really matter. We still would be sent off to Poston even if I remained silent.
3. What would you have done if you were in my shoes?

After sharing his storyboard, Denny asked his classmates what they would have done if they'd been in Koike's position: "How many of you actually would refuse to cooperate with the FBI if you were asked to provide information about your own families, friends, and neighbors?" While many students publicly stated that they were wholeheartedly against "snitches," some also discussed the legal implications of refusing to provide law enforcement with information. Several students recounted chilling examples from their own families' experiences, including being detained, harassed, or surveilled by law enforcement until someone broke under pressure. Denny also pointed out that when under distress and duress, we, as Americans under our current legal system and as imperfect human beings, may make hasty decisions that we later regret, such as "snitching" on another person. Other important topics that arise include whether people who are pressured by law enforcement to provide "information" might embellish certain facts in order to protect themselves or out of fear of retaliation.

Figure 6.2. Sample storyboard (Tsuyoshi Koike).

Reading "The Legend of Miss Sasagawara"

Originally written in 1942, Yamamoto's "The Legend of Miss Sasagawara" (2001) is probably the most well-known short story about the World War II incarceration of Japanese Americans. Yamamoto wrote this masterpiece while detained at Poston. Much of the plot is based on real-life events she witnessed while incarcerated; in it, Yamamoto "plays with narration in a manner familiar to readers of short stories: an adult first-person narrator, recalling childhood scenes, occasionally lapses into the language and perception of childhood" (Streamas, 1997, p. 130).

"Miss Sasagawara" details how an incarcerated Japanese American community develops an obsessive fascination with two new residents: Reverend Sasagawara, a Buddhist priest, and his beautiful adult daughter, Mari Sasagawara. The story is narrated by Kiku, the first-person limited narrator who's presented as a young Japanese American woman in her late teens. An unmarried woman in her late thirties who's also a ballerina, Miss Sasagawara is the frequent source of gossip among the camp residents for her seemingly erratic behaviors, including allegedly ogling young teen-age boys, making periodic public outbursts, or, more commonly, keeping to herself and not socializing with other camp residents. In the story, she's twice committed to an asylum. Until the end of the story, Kiku largely characterizes Mari Sasagawara as someone who's deranged and mentally unstable.

Although the story of "Miss Sasagawara" is just twenty pages long, Yamamoto's complex writing style and the use of certain dated terms might pose some comprehension challenges for students. As a class, we complete a couple of prereading strategies to help scaffold the content. I start by asking a volunteer to read out loud the opening paragraph while the rest of the class follows along:

> Even in that unlikely place of wind, sand, and heat, it was easy to imagine Miss Sasagawara a decorative ingredient of some ballet. Her daily costume, brief and fitting closely to her trifling waist, generously billowing below, and bringing together arrestingly rich colors like mustard yellow and forest green, appeared to have been cut from a coarse textured homespun; her shining hair was so long it wound twice around her head to form a coronet; her face was delicate and pale, with a fine nose, pouting bright mouth, and glittering eyes; and her measured walk said, "Look, I'm *walking!*" as though walking were not a common but a rather special thing to be doing. I first saw her one evening after mess, as she was coming out of the women's latrine going toward her barracks, and after I thought she was out of hearing, I imitated the young men of the Block (No. 33), and gasped, "Wow! How much does *she* weigh?" (p. 20)

After our whole-group reading, I ask students to reread the passage to themselves silently and to circle or highlight words that are unfamiliar. Words they often identify as unfamiliar include *homespun, coronet, latrine*, and *barracks*, which are dated or military-specific terms. Rather than ask students to write out the full definitions of the unfamiliar words, I suggest that they look up the meanings in an online dictionary and jot down a quick one- to three-word definition. Example: Latrine: communal toilet. This activity helps prepare them to make sense of other unfamiliar words they'll run across in the rest of the story.

I also ask students to identify specific patterns they notice in Yamamoto's writing style with examples from the text, as well as questions that occur to them after reading. Following are examples of observations and questions they've come up with, which I write on the board for everyone to view.

1. **Patterns:**
   a. Uses alliteration such as in the line "generously <u>billowing</u> <u>below</u>, and <u>bringing</u> . . ."
   b. Detailed descriptions of Miss Sasagawara's physical appearance using feminine imagery—"her face was delicate and <u>pale</u>, with a fine nose, <u>pouting bright</u> mouth, and <u>glittering</u> eyes . . ."
   c. Excessive use of semicolons when the author describes Miss Sasagawara's appearance. Reads like a run-on sentence.
2. **Questions:**
   a. Who are "the young men of Block (No. 33)?" What's the significance of Block No. 33?
   b. Who's the narrator?
   c. Why does the narrator introduce the main character as "Miss Sasagawara" rather than by her first name?
   d. Why is the narrator obsessed with Miss Sasagawara's physical appearance?

The Causes and Consequences of Community Gossip

I ask students to discuss the following question in pairs or small groups:

1. Why do you think people gossip? Discuss the consequences of gossip to a community as a whole, as well as to the individuals within it. You're welcome to briefly share your own experiences within the context of this question.

Students offer incredible insights about why they think people gossip. They cite boredom, envying another person (which they associate with a gossiper's low self-esteem and personal insecurities), and unresolved conflicts between people. We then dig deeper into the ethical dilemmas of either starting a rumor about another person or passing along gossip that we hear about someone else but didn't actually witness or verify ourselves. Students give many excellent examples of how gossip often leads to defamation of character, hurt feelings, and mistrust in a community. One issue about gossip, for example, is that the person being talked about rarely has the chance to respond to what's being said about her or him. When a community doesn't have the opportunity to hear directly from the person being gossiped about, rumors about that individual often balloon into damaging, false, and hurtful comments. All of these thoughts about gossip help set the stage for analyzing the role of gossip in "Miss Sasagawara" in terms of how it shapes readers' interpretations of different characters' intentions.

In "Miss Sasagawara," Kiku mostly relies on community gossip and other secondhand information from her friend, Elsie Kubo, to make certain claims and harsh judgments about Miss Sasagawara. I ask students to explore evidence from the text to determine whether they find Kiku to be a credible source of information, which later could be used to develop a more robust analysis of how Yamamoto employs point of view in the story. To collect answers, I use Padlet (https://padlet.com/), a digital bulletin board that each student contributes to using images, pictures, and/or text sent from a computer or personal device. Padlet works for either group or individual responses; it's also an ideal tool for eliciting responses from quieter students who may not always feel comfortable speaking up in class. Figure 6.3 highlights sample responses from a group of eleventh-grade students based on the prompt: "With your team, discuss whether or not you believe Kiku is a reliable narrator in her descriptions of Miss Sasagawara.

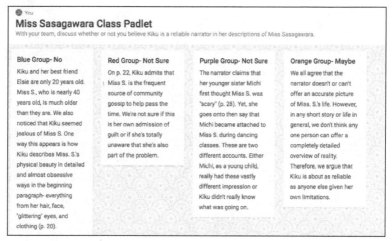

Figure 6.3. Sample Padlet responses on point of view.

Use evidence from the text to explain your team's position." This sample set of responses demonstrates nuanced understandings of the limits of Kiku's point of view. As a follow-up assignment, students are invited to exercise their creativity by rewriting some of the passages from the points of views of the other characters in "Miss Sasagawara."

Writing Assignment: Rewrite portions of "Miss Sasagawara" from the point of view of another character. Try out at least three of the different literary techniques that Yamamoto was famous for (see our prior class notes for examples). Use the guiding questions below to complete this assignment:

1. Select any character except Kiku. For example, you might choose Elsie Kubo, Miss Sasagawara, Reverend Sasagawara, or another major or minor character whose point of view you'd like to explore in greater detail.

> 2. Find a specific moment or scene to rewrite from your character's point of view (identify the page range). For example, your character might respond to a claim, judgment, or observation that Kiku made from her limited point of view.
> 3. Model the descriptive language that Yamamoto uses to construct your person as a round character.
> 4. In class, be prepared to explain why you chose to write about this specific character. Plan on describing the process for how you constructed the new dialogue, moment, or scene, including sharing what you enjoyed about this assignment as well as identifying certain challenges that you experienced.

Students may need help making additional macro-level connections to key themes that Yamamoto explores in "Miss Sasagawara." For instance, Cheung (2000) offers the following ideas (pp. 320–21) for students to analyze further:

1. The ways by which the lack of privacy at Poston perpetuated gossip and gossiping among the Japanese American community.
2. The community's constant scrutiny and surveillance of Miss Sasagawara's body was a microcosm of the White majority's suspicion of Japanese Americans before they were incarcerated.
3. How the Japanese concept of etiquette and manners, especially for women, is gendered. *Enryo* and *gaman* are terms associated with modesty, perseverance, and self-restraint.

Analyzing Gender Roles and Representations of Women
Girls and women in the United States have long responded to and negotiated gendered expectations, roles, and stereotypes. While

there seem to be more progressive attitudes about the advancement of girls and women in twenty-first-century United States, there still are deeply engrained societal expectations regarding how socially desirable females should act, behave, and live. For example, students frequently show me Facebook posts or share gossip magazines that offer sometimes blatant and sometimes subtle critiques or praises of certain female celebrities for their clothing choices or how they style their hair. As students often point out, women who are labeled as desirable, good, and ideal are generally those who not only act and dress in ways considered to be traditionally feminine, but also desire to take on marriage and parenting responsibilities within the context of heterosexual relationships.

Although a bit dated in terms of some of its cultural references, "Miss Sasagawara" includes several themes related to gender identity and sexuality that are relevant to the lives of most twenty-first-century American teenagers. Students who identify as female, male, and/or nonconforming have engaged in brilliant discussions about how independent single women like Miss Sasagawara are often ostracized by others for not conforming to gender stereotypes. Indeed, Miss Sasagawara is portrayed as a complex character who embodies contradictions, such as being fragile yet resilient. She's obviously an imperfect human being, yet she's also held to high standards of perfection by her ethnic community.

Below are discussion questions or essay prompts that could help students further analyze gender identity and stereotypes about women from key scenes in "Miss Sasagawara":

1. Kiku focuses intensely on Miss Sasagawara's physical appearance, from how she dresses to how she walks. Drawing from key dialogue and scenes from the text, analyze and critique the gendered

connotations of Miss Sasagawara's femininity in relation to her physical appearance.

2. Discuss the characterization of Reverend Sasagawara as a father, revered religious figure, and widower.

3. Analyze how Miss Sasagawara's characterization challenges or reinforces common stereotypes about unmarried American women. Find at least three key examples from dialogue, scenes, and textual descriptions in the story to support your analyses.

4. Analyze how Miss Sasagawara's character and the story itself could be seen as challenging but also perpetuating heteronormative and heterosexist societal expectations and norms.

Connections to Other Women Writers

Because Yamamoto's short stories have thematic connections similar to those of more widely taught women authors, teachers may find value in pairing "Miss Sasagawara" with other texts. For example, there are rich parallels between the themes in "The Legend of Miss Sasagawara" and classics such as Kate Chopin's *The Awakening* (1899). The protagonists of both stories, Mari Sasagawara and Edna Pontellier, are round characters who are depicted as flawed human beings. Both protagonists are constructed as independent and strong-minded women who defy gender stereotypes, including expectations that ideal women must be docile, subservient to men, and "well-behaved." At the same time, Miss Sasagawara and Edna are judged harshly by others around them and viewed as eccentrically insane women. Both stories also subtly critique the ways outspoken and resilient women are publicly humiliated and shamed for not confirming to gendered norms.

Parallels could also be drawn between the literature of Yamamoto and that of other women writers, especially American Indians and other writers of color. Prominent Latina writers such as Sandra Cisneros and Roberta Fernández speak to issues that Yamamoto and other Asian American women writers have explored, including how young female protagonists negotiate their gendered and racialized identities in and out of their ethnic communities. Latina and Asian American women writers often explore issues in their writings such as bicultural identity, immigration, language, and race relations in the United States that tend to narrowly focus on the Black–White racial binary. Like Yamamoto, many American Indian women writers and other women of color authors critique traditional gender roles, detail the struggles their families have experienced in light of historical trauma, and highlight the wisdom that community elders, particularly elderly female relatives, transmit across the generations.

The following authors and titles may interest teachers who want to explore comparative lessons on women's literature or who are interested in having students form literature circles to learn more about a specific author:

- **Kate Chopin:** *The Awakening* (1899). Themes—the fate and scrutiny of independent women who defy gendered expectations about marriage, motherhood, and the "well-behaved" woman
- **Sandra Cisneros:** *Woman Hollering Creek and Other Stories* (1991) and *The House on Mango Street* (1984). Themes—negotiating bicultural identity, immigrant experiences from the perspectives of female family members, and women's relationships with men
- **Alma Gómez, Cherríe Moraga, and Mariana Romo-Carmona:** *Cuentos: Stories by Latinas* (1983). Themes—acculturation struggles and identity development among girls and women of color with bicultural backgrounds

■ **Zora Neale Hurston:** *Their Eyes Were Watching God* (1937). Themes—gender roles, jealousy between women, and stereotypes of unmarried women

■ **Toni Morrison:** *The Bluest Eye* (1970) and *Beloved* (1987). Themes—community scrutiny of women, gendered gaze of the female body, and stereotypes of the "mad woman"

■ **Leslie Marmon Silko:** *Ceremony* (1977). Themes—comparing the factors that drove the protagonists (Miss Sasagawara and Tayo) to mental instability, including analyzing gender differences between the characters

Reading Other Japanese American Short Stories

Compared to other genres such as the novel and poetry, short stories that are specifically situated around the Japanese American incarceration during World War II are scarce. Several unpublished short stories written by Japanese Americans while in camp have been preserved in government archives, although most of these hidden gems aren't easily accessible to the public.

The following Japanese American short stories could be comparatively analyzed or paired with one of Yamamoto's works. These stories are available at many public and university libraries and, fortunately, are still in print.

■ **Lonny Kaneko:** "The Shoyu Kid" (1976). This is a somber story about how three Japanese American boys relentlessly bullied a younger boy nicknamed Shoyu Kid (*shoyu* is the Japanese word for soy sauce) who always appeared to be fragile, sick, and vulnerable. They later learn that several of the Shoyu Kid's erratic behaviors resulted from having been sexually molested by a White American camp guard. This short story offers several possibilities for analysis, including the consequences of assimilation, depictions of community surveillance, and linking the World War II incarceration to metaphors of rape and sexual assault. This story may not be appropriate for all classroom settings, as it contains several homophobic slurs and references to child molestation.

- **Toshio Mori:** *Yokohama, California* (2015 Rev. Ed.). Mori's collection includes several interesting short stories about Japanese American experiences that are primarily set before World War II. While detained at the Topaz War Relocation Center in Utah, Mori wrote "Tomorrow Is Coming, Children" the only story in this collection that specifically pertains to the World War II incarceration. While they are detained, a Japanese immigrant grandmother tells her grandchildren about the various hardships she endured since coming to the United States.

- **Wakako Yamauchi:** various short stories from *Songs My Mother Taught Me: Stories, Plays, and Memoir* (1994). "A Veteran of Foreign Wars" offers insights into life after World War II, including the various challenges that Japanese Americans encountered during their reintegration into a White-dominated society. The story focuses on a Japanese American veteran's struggles with amputation and the lingering effects of PTSD. Yamauchi's writing style is especially useful for teaching students about place and setting. A side note: through their shared experiences as detainees at Poston, Yamauchi and Yamamoto became lifelong friends who wrote their stories around Japanese American women protagonists.

7 Connecting Japanese American Literature to Current Events

■■

Ethnic literature empowers teachers to promote an issues-centered approach to learning (Gopalakrishnan, 2010), which encourages students to make connections between a certain text and larger sociopolitical issues. Analyzing the fate of Japanese Americans in the 1940s with parallels to other racialized Americans in the current political climate allows students to critically consider the causes and consequences of racist and xenophobic rhetoric. When I taught John Okada's *No-No Boy* to a group of twelfth graders at a racially diverse urban public high school in 2015, I invited students to identify memorable passages that connect to some type of contemporary moral dilemma or social problem that they're passionate about. They noticed that the public's reaction to the No-No Boys as political dissenters was similar to the ways in which many Americans of color have been ostracized by the general public when they engage in acts of civil disobedience.

During one class period, I asked students to compare the key themes in Okada's *No-No Boy* with the public perceptions of Colin Kaepernick, the African American quarterback from the San Francisco 49ers who's been both criticized and praised for refusing to stand for the US national anthem during this opening-game ritual. Kaepernick had publicly stated that by refusing to stand and instead kneeling during this ritual, he was peacefully protesting the wide-scale mistreatment of African Americans and other people of color as evidenced by the recent police shootings of unarmed African Americans across the nation. The Kaepernick connection to Japanese American dissenters generated a heated debate. Several students in this particular class came from military families. They found Kaepernick's actions to be offensive and unpatriotic. Paul, who identified as Sudanese American and planned to join the US army, stated, "This guy [Kaepernick] clearly has no respect for our country," and several other students nodded in agreement. Terry, who identified as African American and biracial, countered, "Why do you say Kaepernick is disrespectful? He's saying the truth. Look at what's been happening with all of those killings of Black people. He [Kaepernick] is just kneeling. He wasn't hurting anyone." While different students had varied opinions and reactions to Kaepernick's situation and other group or individual forms of protest, they were able to articulate similarities in how different communities and individuals engage in acts of civil disobedience.

Ultimately, conversations such as these provide avenues for students to engage in critical dissent and open discourse while making connections back to the text. In this case, we discussed how historically and currently, men of color who take unpopular stances on significant moral issues, such as Black athletes like Colin Kaepernick and Muhammad Ali or the Japanese American No-No Boys, seem to be more harshly and negatively criticized than White American activists such as the millions of White women who marched in the second-wave feminist movement in the 1960s or those who participated in the Women's March in 2017. Several male students of color wanted to further discuss how men of color who engage in acts of civil disobedience are often ostracized within their own communities and not just by White

Americans—which leads to additional conversations about how factors such as gender and race impact how students experience and read the world around them based on their experiences and identities. In all, reading about Japanese American history and identity through ethnic literature has particular relevance in the literature classroom because:

> this particular segment of history [the incarceration of Japanese Americans] is a crucial slice of ethnic experience in America not only for Japanese-Americans who were profoundly affected by their incarceration, but for all groups wrestling with issues of human rights and problems of ethnic identity. (Harada, 1998, p. 21)

Mashup Activity: Comparative Analysis of Past and Present Forms of Discrimination

To allow students to make their own connections, I invite them to bring current or recent images, magazine articles, newspaper articles, political cartoons, YouTube clips, and other sources to class to compare and contrast their findings about a major social issue that matters to them to the political climate that incarcerated Japanese Americans confronted in the 1940s.

The creative use of multimedia allows students to efficiently summarize and synthesize large bodies of information as they compare and contrast the history of Japanese Americans to other groups that have also experienced legal and societal discrimination such as people who identify as disabled, ethnic/racial minorities, female, LGBTQ, religious minorities, or the working poor. Alone or in groups, students create and share their own mashups that replace traditional in-class presentations.

Mashup Directions: Create a short mashup (no longer than five minutes) that describes how the experiences of a socially marginalized group today have parallels with the treatment of Japanese Americans during World War II. In your mashup:
1. Identify your group.
2. Explain how this group has been legally and/or socially discriminated against. Your mashup should contain at least three distinct examples.
3. Find art, books, images, poems, songs, and/or sound clips that speak to this group's concerns, experiences, or identities.

More Connections with Poetry

Fifty Years

Half a century ago,
we are speaking of another time,
another life.
We are returning to that era of war,
divided loyalties, betrayal,
and incarceration.
Many of us have already gone,
some in fading notoriety,
some with trauma and conflicts
unresolved.

"Fifty Years," a 1992 poem created by critically acclaimed Japanese American playwright Wakako Yamauchi, offers keen insights into how the World War II incarceration of Japanese Americans has remained an "unresolved trauma" for the United States decades after the war ended. Yamauchi was only seventeen years old when her family was incarcerated at the Poston War Relocation

Center in Arizona. The timing of the publication of "Fifty Years" is significant, as it occurred only four years after the passage of the Civil Liberties Act of 1988 that led to government reparations for Japanese American camp survivors. Yamauchi (2000) reiterates that remembering rather than forgetting a traumatic event like the World War II incarceration is an essential step for the United States as a nation to address its unresolved conflicts and problems.

I've used "Fifty Years" to engage students in discussing the politics of remembrance in the US context. The "trauma and conflicts / unresolved" Yamauchi speaks of in her poem suggest that no amount of money could compensate for the losses that Japanese Americans endured during World War II. Her point could be used as a springboard for students to discuss what reparations should look like for other groups, such as African Americans who are the descendants of enslaved Africans and generations of American Indians. "Fifty Years" also speaks to the contested political climate in the 1990s: "We are returning to that era of war, / divided loyalties, betrayal." The early 1990s were rife with civil discord over the Gulf War of 1991–1992 and the 1992 Los Angeles riots. Although the 1990s are history to today's young adults, those events mirror recent acts of civil disobedience, such as the momentum arising from the Black Lives Matter movement in the aftermath of multiple shootings of unarmed African American women and men across the nation, as well as the thousands of Americans who have protested social injustices such as the construction of the infamous Dakota Access oil pipeline and the government's mishandling of the lead-water crisis in Flint, Michigan.

Students also seem to respond well to poems like "Fifty Years" because they connect national concerns about civil liberties, hate crimes, and the consequences of intolerance and wartime hysteria at different moments in American history. We discuss how and why "this lesson [the mistreatment of Japanese Americans during World War II] must be learned and learned and learned again" (Houston & Houston, 2002, p. 188), including grappling with a difficult reality: while some strides have been made since the 1940s, there are still significant challenges in twenty-first-century America around race relations and inequality. We're living in times when activists, citizens, and politicians across ethnic and political lines cite the World War II incarceration of Japanese Americans as a haunting reminder to all Americans that our nation can't afford to repeat the mistake of denying a group of people their civil rights due to bigotry, fear, or in the name of national security—not if the United States is to serve as the world's exemplar of democracy and freedom.

Final Reflections

The incarceration of Japanese Americans in the 1940s is one of the most powerful reminders about what's at stake when the civil rights of *all* Americans aren't guaranteed or protected. Japanese American literature focused on this historical moment provides young adults with readable and relatable ways to learn about an event that's often elided in American history while making their own connections to timely and urgent social issues that matter to them. During an interview with comedian Jon Stewart in 2014, Japanese American actor George Takei summarized what his father told him after the end of World War II: "Our democracy is a people's democracy. And it can be as great as people can be, but it is also as fallible as people are" ("Actor George Takei," 2014, n.p.). Indeed, young adults tend to be highly aware of and sympathetic to the concept of fairness, especially when it directly applies to their own situations. The challenge, then, is to encourage all youth and all Americans to collectively insist on freedom and justice for all and not just some.

Annotated Bibliography

■ ■

A Boolean web search of "Japanese American literature" will yield more than 1.75 million results, including annotated bibliographies, author websites, course syllabi, and hundreds of peer-reviewed journal articles in the humanities and social sciences. Also widely available are government documents related to the World War II experience of Japanese Americans, such as those found through the National Park Service, and teacher-created WebQuests, including supplements such as interdisciplinary lesson and unit plans. Included here is an annotated bibliography of select sources for teachers about the World War II incarceration that could supplement literature-based units. Although by no means comprehensive, this list points English teachers to key primary and secondary sources they may wish to read on their own, share with their students, or both.

Asian American Literature

CHAN, JEFFREY PAUL, FRANK CHIN, LAWSON FUSAO INADA, AND SHAWN WONG. *The Big AIIIEEEEE! An Anthology of Chinese American and Japanese American Literature.* New York: Meridian, 1991. [The original collection, simply titled *Aiiieeeee!,* was published in 1974.]

In this thick collection, the editors offer an emotional critique of Asian American writers who they believe have "sold out" to White American audiences by writing stories that depict Asian Americans in one-dimensional and racially stereotypical ways. Particular criticism is directed at critically acclaimed authors such as Maxine Hong Kingston, the author of *Woman Warrior,* whom Chin in particular accuses of producing literary works that are culturally inaccurate, inauthentic, and insensitive. While controversial, this anthology offers readers with critical insights about the politics of representation in Asian American literature. It also includes selections of works by Asian American writers whose writings challenge stereotypical representations of Asian Americans.

KIM, ELAINE H. *Asian American Literature: An Introduction to the Writings and Their Social Context.* Philadelphia: Temple University Press, 1984.

The first known academic book that introduces readers to works written by Chinese American, Filipina/Filipino American, Japanese American, and Korean American authors includes interviews with well-known Asian American writers, as well as literary analyses and interpretations of select works. The book also offers important historical, political, and social contexts for reading Asian American literature.

WONG, SHAWN. *Asian American Literature: A Brief Introduction and Anthology.* New York: Longman, 1996.

Written by a critically acclaimed Chinese American author and scholar, this thick anthology is frequently used in introductory Asian American studies and ethnic studies courses across US colleges and universities. It's organized chronologically by genre, and includes a separate thematic table of contents that allows teachers to quickly create well-sequenced lesson and unit plans. Wong includes a diverse range of writings by Asian Americans, including autobiographies, dramas, novels, memoirs, poetry, and short stories, and draws from both classic and contemporary works in Asian American literature. Asian American writers of different ethnic groups and nationalities are represented, enabling readers to appreciate the diversity within the Asian American community.

Documentaries and Films about the World War II Incarceration

442: Live with Honor, Die with Dignity. Written and directed by Junichi Suzuki, 2010. (97 min.)

The most highly decorated unit during World War II, the 442nd Regimental Combat Team was a racially segregated unit comprising of Japanese American men who volunteered for service. This film narrates the contributions and sacrifices of these soldiers while also spotlighting the disturbing irony that these men were fighting for freedom when their own people were imprisoned for a crime they hadn't committed. It includes interviews with prominent Japanese American community leaders, including the late Senator Daniel Inouye and actor-activist George Takei.

Children of the Camps. Produced and co-written by Satsuki Ina, 1999. (57 min.) [Available for purchase from the Center for Asian American Media.]

With an overview narrated by Japanese American activist and writer Lawson Fusao Inada, who wrote a poem similarly titled "Children of Camp," from his poetry collection *Drawing the Line* (1997), this documentary presents the stories of six Japanese Americans—Howard Ikemoto, Marion Kanemoto, Bessie Masuda, Richard Tatsuo Nagaoka, Ruth Okimoto, and Toru Saito. All of the participants were either born in camp or incarcerated during World War II as children or young adults. The format is a three-day community education workshop facilitated by Japanese American camp survivor Satsuki Ina, a marriage and family therapist and professor emerita at California State University, Sacramento. Workshop participants reflect on their traumatic childhood experiences, sharing how their treatment during the war created lifelong trauma for themselves and their families. An accompanying website includes free resources such as a teacher's guide: www.pbs.org/childofcamp/resources/index.html.

Citizen Tanouye. Co-directed and co-produced by Robert Horsting and Craig Yahata, 2008. (58 min.)

Sgt. Ted Tanouye was a Japanese American veteran of the 442nd Regimental Combat Team whose family was incarcerated at the Jerome and Rohwer concentration camps in Arkansas during World War II. Tanouye was a 1938 graduate of Torrance High School in California. Years later, students at Torrance decided to learn more about Tanouye's story and how World War II impacted their community. For this film project, students conducted extensive research by analyzing primary sources such as local newspapers and the school's yearbooks, interviewing World War II veterans, and reflecting on how Tanouye's life intersected with their own experiences as young bicultural Americans.

Conscience and the Constitution. Produced, directed, and written by Frank Abe, 2000. (57 min.)

This documentary chronicles the real-life story of Frank Emi and other Japanese American members of the Heart Mountain Fair Play Committee, a group of draft-eligible Japanese American men who pushed for draft resistance because their families were illegally incarcerated at the Heart Mountain Relocation Center in Wyoming, one of the ten concentration camps built to detain Japanese Americans. The men all refused the draft during World War II in what has long been considered one of the riskiest acts of civil disobedience in Asian American history, especially during their generation. Emi and other resisters were eventually prosecuted as criminals by the US government, sent to jail for two years, and ultimately ostracized by other Japanese Americans who felt their decision to resist the draft was unpatriotic. The film illustrates a little-known event in Japanese American history that continues to divide the Japanese American community. It pairs well with lessons on Lawson Fusao Inada's writings or reading John Okada's *No-No Boy.* The film's website, RESISTORS .COM (http://resisters.com/), contains a wealth of resources for teachers such as a viewer's guide and video clips.

Days of Waiting: The Life and Art of Estelle Ishigo. Produced, directed, and written by Steven Okazaki, 2000. (28 min.)

Estelle Peck Ishigo, a White American woman, refused to allow her Japanese American husband to go to camp alone during World War II. This documentary focuses on her story as one of the few White Americans incarcerated with Japanese Americans during the war. Ishigo was first incarcerated in Pomona, California, before being relocated to Heart Mountain, Wyoming. Ishigo meticulously documents the dark side of camp life through artwork, including paintings and sketches, as well as personal photos. Her story is particularly unique because antimiscegenation laws were in place during the 1940s that legally barred interracial marriages, and also ties into contemporary discussions about why relationships between Asian American men and White American women are still uncommon in twenty-first-century America.

Passing Poston: An American Story. Directed by Joe Fox and James Nubile, 2008. (105 min.)

More than 18,000 Japanese Americans were incarcerated in Poston, Arizona, during World War II. *Passing Poston* traces the stories of four of those individuals—Mary Higashi, Ruth Okimoto, Kiyo Sato, and Leon Uyeda. The Poston detention camp was built on the Colorado River Indian Reservation that was already inhabited by the Chemehuevi and the Mohave. The US government used Japanese Americans as cheap labor to build schools, develop the reservation's infrastructure, and try out experimental farming techniques that would later be used by the Hopi and Navajo tribes. When Japanese Americans left Poston after the end of World War II, American Indians settled into the barracks. This documentary is an excellent resource for teaching about the intersections between the racialized historical experiences of Hopi, Navajo, and Japanese Americans. It also pairs well with Lawson Fusao Inada's poems that analyze the parallels between Japanese American and American Indian cultural identities and histories.

Time of Fear. Directed and written by Sue Williams, 2005. (60 min.)

This documentary highlights a relatively unexamined aspect of the Japanese American incarcerations: 16,000 Japanese Americans were sent to two camps in remote areas of southeast Arkansas, a place rife with long-standing and tense race relations, particularly between Blacks and Whites. Local citizens are interviewed, including African American locals and Japanese American camp survivors.

Internet Resources

Denshō
www.densho.org/

Denshō is a nonprofit organization based in Seattle that documents the oral histories of Japanese Americans. Denshō includes more than 12,000 historical images and 1,400 hours of interviews and other primary sources from Japanese Americans and others who were impacted by the World War II incarceration. It also includes a multimedia encyclopedia and provides access to a range of primary and secondary sources.

Discover Nikkei
www.discovernikkei.org/en/

The term *Nikkei* refers to all persons of Japanese ancestry who live outside of Japan. Discover Nikkei, sponsored by the Japanese American National Museum, focuses on the lives of Japanese migrants and their descendants across the world. Discover Nikkei is the world's most comprehensive source of information on Japanese people of the diaspora. This ambitious project includes the experiences of a diverse range of *Nikkei* in North America, South America, and other regions of the world, including how the World War II era impacted different subgroups of *Nikkei*. It also includes a wealth of primary sources, including databases, interviews, lesson plans, local events, and writings by *Nikkei* across different generations and nationalities.

Japanese American Citizens League (JACL)
www.jacl.org/

Founded in 1929, JACL is the oldest Asian American civil rights organization in the United States. The site outlines JACL's main priorities—advocacy, education, leadership, and public policy—and includes updates on major events such as conferences and conventions. The website also contains access to free or low-cost curriculum guides and lesson plans for classroom teachers. Local JACL chapters are also often able to visit K–12 and university classrooms to provide free lectures and workshops about Japanese American experiences during World War II.

Japanese American National Museum (JANM)
www.janm.org/

Located in Little Tokyo near downtown Los Angeles, JANM opened its doors in 1992 to promote public awareness of Japanese American culture, histories, and identities. JANM's site contains more than 60,000 primary sources such as images of artifacts, documents, and photographs, all available to the public. The website also provides updates on upcoming conferences, events, and exhibitions.

The Pacific Citizen
www.pacificcitizen.org/

The Pacific Citizen is a JACL-sponsored national news source that was originally geared toward a Japanese American readership and today is meant to be more inclusive of the diverse pan-Asian Pacific American community. It contains digital archives of back issues dating to the 1930s. It's a great resource for students conducting historical research or those eager to learn more about social issues that have impacted a more culturally, ethnically, and linguistically Asian Pacific American community over the past several decades.

Works Cited

ACTOR GEORGE TAKEI SHARES FAMILY'S STORY OF WWII INTERNMENT. (2014, July 24). *NBC News.* Retrieved from http://www.nbcnews.com/news/asian-america/actor-george-takei-shares-familys-story-wwii-internment-n163961

ALEXIE, S. (2009). *War dances.* New York: Grove Press.

ANGELOU, M. (1969). *I know why the caged bird sings.* New York: Random House.

ASSOCIATION FOR JAPANESE LANGUAGE TEACHING (AJALT). (1996). *Japanese for busy people: Kana workbook.* New York: Kodansha International USA.

BEGAY, S. (1995). *Navajo: Visions and voices across the Mesa.* New York: Scholastic.

BRIDEGAM, M., & SHIGEKUNI, L. (2015a). Filming "Farewell to Manzanar" at Tule Lake: Seeing one camp in another—part 1. *Discover Nikkei.* Retrieved from http://www.discovernikkei.org/en/journal/2015/5/19/farewell-to-manzanar-1/

BRIDEGAM, M., & SHIGEKUNI, L. (2015b). Filming "Farewell to Manzanar" at Tule Lake: Seeing one camp in another—part 2. *Discover Nikkei.* Retrieved from http://www.discovernikkei.org/en/journal/2015/5/19/farewell-to-manzanar-2/

BRIDEGAM, M., & SHIGEKUNI, L. (2015c). Filming "Farewell to Manzanar" at Tule Lake: Seeing one camp in another—part 3. *Discover Nikkei.* Retrieved from http://www.discovernikkei.org/en/journal/2015/5/19/farewell-to-manzanar-3/

BROWN, R. (2007). Full circle: An interview with Lawson Fusao Inada. *The Museletter, XXVIII*(1), 1–26.

BRUCHAC, J. (n.d.). Select poems. Retrieved from http://josephbruchac.com/

BURT, R. (2010). Interning America's colonial history: The anthologies and poetry of Lawson Fusao Inada. *MELUS, 35*(3) 105–30.

CHAN, J. P., CHIN, F., INADA, L.F., & WONG, S. (1991). Introduction. In J. P. Chan, F. Chin, L. F. Inada, & S. Wong, *The big aiiieeeee! An anthology of Chinese American and Japanese American literature* (pp. xi–xvi). New York: Meridian.

CHANG, Y. (2010). *Writing the ghetto: Class, authorship, and the Asian American ethnic enclave.* New Brunswick, NJ: Rutgers University Press.

CHEUNG, K. K. (1996). Reading between the syllables: Hisaye Yamamoto's 'Seventeen syllables and other stories.' In J. R. Maitino & D. R. Peck (Eds.), *Teaching American ethnic literatures: Nineteen essays* (pp. 313–25). Albuquerque: University of New Mexico Press.

CHEUNG, K. K. (2000). Hisaye Yamamoto and Wakako Yamauchi: Interview by King-Kok Cheung. In K. K. Cheung (Ed.), *Words matter: Conversations with Asian American writers* (pp. 343–82). Honolulu: University of Hawai'i Press.

CHIN, F. (1976). Open letter to John Korty. *Mother Jones, 1*(3), 4.

CHIN, F. (1991). Come all ye Asian American writers of the real and the fake. In. J. P. Chan, F. Chin, L. F. Inada, & S. Wong, *The big aiiieeeee! An anthology of Chinese American and Japanese American literature* (pp. 1–92). New York: Meridian.

CHIU, S. S. (1997). Reorienting the English classroom: Asian American writers in the canon. *English Journal, 86*(8), 30–3.

CHOPIN, K. (1993). *The awakening.* New York: Dover Publications. (Original work published 1899)

CISNEROS, S. (1984). *The house on Mango Street.* Houston: Arte Público Press.

CISNEROS, S. (1991). *Woman hollering creek and other stories.* New York: Random House.

CROW, C. (1987). A *MELUS* interview: Hisaye Yamamoto. *MELUS, 14*(1), 73-84.

DANIELS, R. (1998). Incarcerating Japanese Americans: An atrocity revisited. *Peace & Change, 23*(2), 117–34.

DANIELS, R. (2002). Incarceration of the Japanese Americans: A sixty-year perspective. *History Teacher, 35*(3), 297–310.

DANIELS, R. (2005). Words do matter: A note on inappropriate terminology and the incarceration of the Japanese Americans. In L. Fiset & G. M. Nomura (Eds.), *Nikkei in the Pacific Northwest: Japanese Americans and Japanese Canadians in the twentieth century* (pp. 183–207). Seattle: Center for the Study of the Pacific Northwest/University of Seattle Press.

DISCOVER NIKKEI. (n.d.). Jeanne Wakatsuki Houston [Webpage]. *Discover Nikkei*. Retrieved from http://www.discovernikkei.org/en/interviews/profiles/61/

ENDO, R. (2009). Complicating culture and difference: Situating Asian American youth identities in Lisa Yee's *Millicent Min, girl genius* and *Stanford Wong flunks big-time*. *Children's Literature in Education, 40*(3), 235–49.

ENDO, R. (2012). Mis/representations of Asian/Americans in the curricula: Perspectives from second-generation Japanese American youth. *International Journal of Multicultural Education, 14*(1), 1–18.

ESPIRITU, Y. L. (1992). *Asian American panethnicity: Bridging institutions and identities.* Philadelphia: Temple University Press.

FERTIG, B., & KHAN, Y. (2016). How to talk about the election with students. *School Book*. Retrieved from https://www.wnyc.org/story/students-teachers-presidential-election-trump-clinton/

FILM REVIEW. (n.d.). Duke University's Thompson Writing Center, Durham, NC. Retrieved from https://twp.duke.edu/sites/twp.duke.edu/files/file-attachments/film-review-1.original.pdf

FRANK, A. (1952). *The diary of a young girl.* Amsterdam: Contact Publishing. (Original work published 1947)

FRIEDSON, A. M. (1984). No more farewells: An interview with Jeanne and John Houston. *Biography, 7*(1), 50–73.

FUGITA, S. (1999). Jeanne Wakatsuki Houston. In H. Kim (Ed.), *Distinguished Asian Americans: A biographical dictionary* (pp. 121–23). Westport, CT: Greenwood Press.

GÓMEZ, A., MORAGA, C., & ROMO-CARMONA, M. (1983). *Cuentos: Stories by Latinas.* New York: Kitchen Table/Women of Color Press.

GOPALAKRISHNAN, A. (2010). *Multicultural children's literature: A critical issues approach.* Thousand Oaks, CA: SAGE.

GULLO, K. (n.d.). Easing into memoirs. *Write It.* New York: Scholastic. Retrieved from http://teacher.scholastic.com/writeit/memoir/teacher/easing.htm

HARADA, V. H. (1998). Caught between two worlds: Themes of family, community, and ethnic identity in Yoshiko Uchida's works for children. *Children's Literature in Education, 29*(1), 19–30.

HARRIS, V. J. (2003). The complexity of debates about multicultural literature and cultural authenticity. In D. L. Fox & K. G. Short (Eds.), *Stories matter: Cultural authenticity in children's literature* (pp. 116--34). Urbana, IL: National Council of Teachers of English.

HENSLER, P., WITH HOUSTON, J. W. (1984). *Don't cry, it's only thunder.* Garden City, NY: Doubleday.

HERNÁNDEZ, D. (2015). *A cup of water under my bed: A memoir.* Boston: Beacon Press.

HISAYE YAMAMOTO. (n.d.a). *Densho Encyclopedia.* Retrieved from http://encyclopedia.densho.org/Hisaye_Yamamoto/

HISAYE YAMAMOTO. (n.d.b). *Densho Encyclopedia.* Interview. Retrieved from http://encyclopedia.densho.org/Hisaye%20Yamamoto/

HOUSTON, J. D., & HOUSTON, J. W. (1985). *One can think about life after the fish is in the canoe: And other coastal sketches beyond Manzanar: Views of Asian American womanhood.* Santa Barbara, CA: Capra Press.

HOUSTON, J. W. (2003). *The legend of fire horse woman.* New York: Kensington Books.

HOUSTON, J. W., & HOUSTON, J. D. (2002). *Farewell to Manzanar: A true story of Japanese American experience during and after the World War II internment.* Boston: Houghton Mifflin. (Original work published 1973)

HURSTON, Z. N. (1937). *Their eyes were watching god.* Philadelphia: J. B. Lippincott.

INADA, L. F. (1971). *Before the war: Poems as they happened.* New York: Morrow.

INADA, L. F. (1993). *Legends from camp: Poems.* Minneapolis: Coffee House Press.

INADA, L. F. (1997). *Drawing the line: Poems.* Minneapolis: Coffee House Press.

INADA, L. F. (Ed.) (2000). *Only what we could carry: The Japanese American internment experience*. Berkeley, CA: Heyday Books.

INADA, L. F., KIKUMURA, A., WORTHINGTON, M., & AZUMA, E. (1993). *In this great land of freedom: The Japanese pioneers of Oregon*. Los Angeles: Japanese American National Museum.

IWATSUKI, S. (2000). Untitled poem. In L. F. Inada (Ed.) *Only what we could carry: The Japanese American internment experience* (p. 388). Berkeley, CA: Heyday Books.

JAGO, C. (2006). *Judith Ortiz Cofer in the classroom: "A woman in front of the sun."* Urbana, IL: National Council of Teachers of English.

JAPANESE AMERICAN CITIZENS LEAGUE. (2005). *A troubling legacy: Anti-Asian sentiment in America*. San Francisco: Japanese American Citizens League. Retrieved from https://jacl.org/wordpress/wp-content/uploads/2015/01/A-Troubling-Legacy.pdf

JAPANESE AMERICAN CITIZENS LEAGUE, POWER OF WORDS II COMMITTEE (2013). *Power of words handbook: A guide to language about Japanese Americans in World War II: Understanding euphemisms and preferred terminology.* San Francisco: Japanese American Citizens League. Retrieved from https://jacl.org/wordpress/wp-content/uploads/2015/08/Power-of-Words-Rev.-Term.-Handbook.pdf

KANEKO, L. (1976). The Shoyu Kid. *Amerasia Journal, 3*(2), 1–19.

KORTY, J. (Producer). (1976). *Farewell to Manzanar* [Motion picture]. United States: NBC Universal.

KROGSTAD, J. M., & FRY, R. (2014). Dept. of Ed. projects public schools will be "majority minority" this fall. Washington, DC: Pew Research Center. Retrieved from: http://www.pewresearch.org/fact-tank/2014/08/18/u-s-public-schools-expected-to-be-majority-minority-starting-this-fall/

LAWSON FUSAO INADA. (n.d.). *Denshō Encyclopedia*. Retrieved from http://encyclopedia.densho.org/Lawson%20Fusao%20Inada/

LEE, G. (2003, June 1). The forgotten revolution. *Hyphen Magazine*. Retrieved from http://hyphenmagazine.com/magazine/issue-1-premiere-summer-2003/forgotten-revolution

MAKI, M. T., KITANO, H. H. L., & BERTHOLD, S. M. (1999). *Achieving the impossible dream: How Japanese Americans obtained redress*. Urbana, IL: University of Illinois Press.

MAY IS ASIAN/PACIFIC AMERICAN HERITAGE MONTH. (2012). *Curriculum Review, 51*(8), 11.

MCDONALD, D. R., & NEWMAN, K. (1980). Relocation and dislocation: The writings of Hisaye Yamamoto and Wakako Yamauchi. *MELUS, 7*(3), 21–38.

MCINTOSH, P. (1989, July/August). White privilege: Unpacking the invisible knapsack. *Peace and Freedom Magazine,* 10–12.

MICHAELS, C. (2010, October). Historical trauma and microaggressions: A framework for culturally-based practice. *Child Welfare Series.* Minneapolis: University of Minnesota Extension, Children, Youth & Family Consortium *eReview.* Retrieved from http://www.extension.umn.edu/family/cyfc/our-programs/ereview/docs/cmhereviewOct10.pdf

MORI, T. (2015). *Yokohama, California.* Seattle: University of Washington Press. (Original work published in 1949)

MORRISON, T. (1970). *The bluest eye.* New York: Holt, Rinehart & Winston.

MORRISON, T. (1987). *Beloved.* New York: Alfred A. Knopf.

MOSER, L. T. (2001). Jeanne Wakatsuki Houston (1935-) and James D. Houston (1934-). In G. Huang (Ed.), *Asian American autobiographers: A bio-bibliographical critical sourcebook* (pp. 127–33). Westport, CT: Greenwood Press.

MURA, D. (2005). *Turning Japanese: Memoirs of a Sansei.* New York: Grove Press.

MYLORD, L. (2010, October 6). Racism in post-war America: Not a matter of black or white. *Discover Nikkei.* Retrieved from http://www.discovernikkei.org/en/journal/2010/10/6/racism-in-post-war-america/

NATIONAL GOVERNORS ASSOCIATION CENTER FOR BEST PRACTICES (NGA Center), and Council of Chief State School Officers (CCSSO). (2010). *Common Core State Standards for English Language Arts & Literacy in History/Social Studies, Science, and Technical Subjects.* Washington, DC.

NATIONAL PARK SERVICE. (2004). A history of American Indians in California: HISTORIC SITES. National Park Service. Retrieved from https://www.nps.gov/parkhistory/online_books/5views/5views1h11.htm

NEWMAN, E. (2012, January 16). The actors' perspective. *Discover Nikkei.* Retrieved from http://www.discovernikkei.org/en/journal/2012/1/16/actors-perspective/

NGAI, M. M. (2005). *Impossible subjects: Illegal aliens and the making of modern America*. Princeton, NJ: Princeton University Press.

OBAMA, B. (1995). *Dreams from my father: A story of race and inheritance*. New York: Times Books.

OKADA, J. (1957). *No-no boy*. Rutland, VT: C. E. Tuttle.

OKAMURA, R. Y. (1976a). "Farewell to Manzanar": A case of subliminal racism. *Amerasia Journal, 3*(2), 143–48.

OKAMURA, R. Y. (1976b). Open letter to John Korty. *Mother Jones, 1*(3), 4–5.

OKUBO, M. (2003). *Citizen 13660*. Seattle: University of Washington Press. (Original work published 1946)

PARK, J. (2015). Asian American poetry. In C. Parikh & D. Y. Kim (Eds.), *The Cambridge companion to Asian American literature* (pp. 101–13). New York: Cambridge University Press.

Q&A WITH AUTHOR JEANNE WAKATSUKI HOUSTON. (2012, March). *California Humanities*. Retrieved from http://www.calhum.org/news/blog/q-a-with-author-jeanne-wakatsuki-houston

RAYSON, A. (1987). Beneath the mask: Autobiographies of Japanese-American women. *MELUS, 14*(1), 43–57.

ROBINSON, G. (2012, March 14). The great unknown and the unknown great: The life and times of Hisaye Yamamoto: Writer, activist, speaker. *Discover Nikkei*. Retrieved from http://www.discovernikkei.org/en/journal/2012/3/14/hisaye-yamamoto/

SATO, G. K. (2002). Lawson Fusao Inada. In G. Huang & E. S. Nelson (Eds.), *Asian-American poets: A bio-bibliographical critical sourcebook* (pp. 145–57). Westport, CT: Greenwood Press.

SCALES, P. (2006). 15 young-adult classics. *Book Links, 15*(6), 54-5.

SHAKUR, A. (1987). *Assata: An autobiography*. Chicago: Zed Books.

SHEA, R. H., & WILCHECK, D. L. (2005). *Amy Tan in the classroom: "The art of invisible strength."* Urbana, IL: National Council of Teachers of English.

SILKO, L. M. (1977). *Ceremony*. New York: Viking.

SIX-WORD MEMOIRS CAN SAY IT ALL. (2008, February 26). *CBS News*. Retrieved from http://www.cbsnews.com/news/six-word-memoirs-can-say-it-all/

THE INCARCERATION OF JAPANESE AMERICANS IN THE 1940S

SONE, M. I. (2014). *Nisei daughter.* Seattle: University of Washington Press. (Original work published 1952)

SOUTHERN OREGON HISTORICAL SOCIETY. (n.d.) Inada, Lawson Fusao [Webpage]. Retrieved from http://www.sohs.org/content/inada-lawson-fusao

SUZUKI, P. T. (1986). The University of California Japanese evacuation and resettlement study, a prolegomenon. *Dialectical Anthropology, 10*(3/4), 189–213.

TAKAKI, R. (1989). *Strangers from a different shore: A history of Asian Americans.* Boston: Little, Brown.

TERMINOLOGY. (n.d.). *Denshō Encyclopedia.* Retrieved from https://densho.org/terminology/

THALHEIMER, A. N. (1999). Asian American literature. [Review of *Seventeen syllables and other short stories*]. *MELUS, 24*(4), 177–79.

THOMAS, A. (August 2008). How to write your own memoir. *O, The Oprah Magazine.*

TRAUMA. (n.d.). *Psychology Topics.* Washington, DC: American Psychological Association. Retrieved from http://www.apa.org/topics/trauma/

TUAN, M. (1998). *Forever foreigners or honorary whites? The Asian ethnic experience today.* New Brunswick, NJ: Rutgers University Press.

WAKIDA, P. (n.d.). Farewell to Manzanar (book). *Denshō Encyclopedia.* Retrieved from http://encyclopedia.densho.org/Farewell%20to%20 Manzanar%20%28book%29/#cite_ref-ftnt_ref1_0-

WATKINS, R. (2012). *Black power, Yellow power, and the making of revolutionary identities.* Jackson, MS: University Press of Mississippi.

WEGLYN, M. (1996). *Years of infamy: The untold story of America's concentration camps.* Seattle: University of Washington Press (Original book published 1976).

WIXON, V. (n.d.). Lawson Fusao Inada (1938-). *The Oregon Encyclopedia.* Retrieved from http://oregonencyclopedia.org/articles/inada_lawson_fusao_1938_/#.V59k1Y594U0

WONG, N. (2000). Can't tell. In L. F. Inada (Ed.), *Only what we could carry: The Japanese American internment experience* (pp. 51–52). Berkeley, CA: Heyday Books.

Woo, E. (2011, February 13). Hisaye Yamamoto dies at 89; writer of Japanese American stories. *Los Angeles Times*. Retrieved from http://www.latimes.com/local/obituaries/la-me- hisaye-yamamoto-20110213-story.html

Yamamoto, H. (2001). *Seventeen syllables and other stories* (Rev. and Exp.). New Brunswick, NJ: Rutgers University Press. (Original work published 1988)

Yamamoto, J. K. (2011). A new beginning for "Farewell to Manzanar." *Rafu Shimpo*. Retrieved from http://www.rafu.com/2011/10/a-new-beginning-for-farewell-to-manzanar/

Yamauchi, W. (1994). *Songs my mother taught me: Stories, plays, and memoir*. New York: Feminist Press at CUNY.

Yamauchi, W. (2000). "Fifty years." In L. F. Inada (Ed.) *Only what we could carry: The Japanese American internment experience* (p. 388). Berkeley, CA: Heyday Books. (Original work published 1992)

Digital Literacy Tools for the Classroom

Mashups for Education: http://mashupsforeducation.weebly.com/mashup-tools.html

MindMup: www.mindmup.com

Padlet: https://padlet.com/

PBS Learning Media Storyboard: http://www.pbslearningmedia.org/tools/storyboard/

StoryboardThat: http://www.storyboardthat.com/

TodaysMeet (backchannel): https://todaysmeet.com/

Author

■■■■■■■■■■■■■■■■■■■■■■■■■■■■■■■■■

Rachel Endo is dean and professor in the School of Education at the University of Washington Tacoma. She has worked with learners of all ages in Illinois, Minnesota, and Nebraska for more than fifteen years. She has led dozens of institutes, professional learning communities, seminars, and workshops for aspiring and current preK–12 educators, as well as teacher  educators and university faculty in English departments, on curricular and instructional strategies for integrating ethnic studies into their courses.

Endo is committed to advancing causes related to improving educational access, equity, and opportunities for historically underrepresented and underserved communities, families, and learners. A first-generation college student and alumna of the University of Nebraska at Omaha's TRIO Project Achieve program, she went on to obtain an MPA in public management, an MA in secondary education, and a graduate certificate in instructional technology. Her PhD in language and literacy education is from the University of Illinois at Urbana–Champaign.

This book was composed by Barbara Frazier in Berkeley and Interstate.

Typefaces used on the cover include Avenir Next and Avenir Next Condensed.

The book was printed on 50-lb. White Offset paper by King Printing Company, Inc.